Facebook® Marketing

Designing Your Next Marketing Campaign

Justin R. Levy

800 East 96th Street
Indianapolis, Indiana 46240 USA

Facebook Marketing

© Copyright 2010 by Pearson Education, Inc.

ISBN-13: 978-07897-4321-3

0-7897-4321-3

Library of Congress Cataloging-in-Publication Data:
Levy, Justin R. (Justin Robert)
   Facebook marketing : designing your next marketing campaign /
Justin R. Levy.
      p. cm.
   ISBN-13: 978-0-7897-4321-3
   ISBN-10: 0-7897-4321-3
   1.   Internet marketing. 2.   Internet advertising. 3.   Facebook
(Electronic resource)
4.   Social networks--Computer network resources.   I. Title.
   HF5415.1265.L4813 2010
   658.8'72--dc22

          2010005894

Printed in the United States of America

Third Printing: January 2011

Associate Publisher
Greg Wiegand

Acquisitions Editor
Loretta Yates

Development Editor
Kevin Howard

Managing Editor
Kristy Hart

Project Editors
Jovana San Nicolas-Shirley
Anne Goebel

Copy Editor
Apostrophe Editing
Services

Indexer
Erika Millen

Proofreader
Leslie Joseph

Publishing Coordinator
Cindy Teeters

Cover Designer
Anne Jones

Compositor
Jake McFarland

Trademarks

Warning and Disclaimer

Bulk Sales

Que Publishing offers excellent discounts on this book when ordered in quantity for bulk purchases or special sales. For more information, please contact

    U.S. Corporate and Government Sales
    1-800-382-3419
    corpsales@pearsontechgroup.com

For sales outside of the U.S., please contact

    International Sales
    international@pearson.com

CONTENTS AT A GLANCE

TABLE OF CONTENTS

About the Author

Justin R. Levy is the Director of Business Development, Marketing, and Client Relations of New Marketing Labs, a new media marketing agency. In this role Justin helps large and mid-sized businesses navigate the unknown seas of new media marketing including how to use social media tools, blogs, community platforms, and listening tools to drive business value. Justin and his team help their clients move the needles that they care about moving using these new and emerging resources. Justin has worked with brands such as Sony, PepsiCo, Microsoft, Citrix Online, Molson Coors, SAS, and several other big brand partners.

When not busy with New Marketing Labs, Justin is partner and general manager of Caminito Argentinean Steakhouse, located in Massachusetts. Through the use of social media marketing techniques, Justin has successfully grown his steakhouse at least 20 percent in sales every month for more than 24 months straight. Because of this success, Justin and Caminito have been featured in multiple business and marketing books and profiled by some of the most successful marketing blogs in the world.

Justin writes and creates all types of media at justinrlevy.com, which is listed as one of the top 350 marketing blogs worldwide according to *AdAge* and top 5,000 blogs worldwide according to Technorati. Justin is founder and editor of primecutsblog.com, a blog focusing on teaching readers cooking techniques, tips, and recipes, and the editor-in-chief and a contributor for several other blogs on behalf of his clients.

Justin received a master's degree in Homeland Security from the University of Connecticut and dual undergraduate degrees in sociology and criminal justice from the University of Hartford.

Dedication

This book is dedicated to my beautiful wife, Laura. Without her support, none of this would be possible.

Acknowledgments

Thank you to Loretta Yates and everyone at Pearson Education who was patient, encouraging, and true professionals to work with to bring this book to life.

Thank you to the entire team at New Marketing Labs for always supporting my ambitious goals, especially Chris Brogan. Chris, you have been an amazing mentor, friend, and colleague.

A special thanks to all the great partners that I've had the honor of working with at New Marketing Labs. The experiences that I've had working with each of you have provided lifelong lessons, experiences, and friendships.

Thank you to Joseph Gionfriddo for being an amazing best friend and partner to work with and my entire staff at Caminito Argentinean Steakhouse for working as hard as they do on a daily basis to help in our continued success.

Although this book is dedicated to my wife Laura, it's only appropriate that she is acknowledged here as well. You have had a larger impact on my life than any card, bunch of flowers, or gift can ever express. I am blessed to have a wife as beautiful, smart, loving, caring, understanding, and supportive as you are. I love you.

To my mom and dad, who unfortunately I lost way too early in life: I hope that I've made you proud. You are the force looking over my shoulder that has kept pushing me for the past 10 years since you were taken away from me. I love and miss both of you!

Words can never express my gratitude to Laura's family, especially her parents, Jim and Lynne Pasternack. You have always treated me like family, and you have filled a void that had been torn open from the loss of my parents. You provide a model for what the word "family" truly means. Thank you.

To my grandparents, Santo and Norma Lasorsa, and my uncles, Stephen and David Lasorsa, for always being there. Your guidance and support over the years has had an immeasurable impact on who I've become.

To everyone who has supported me over the years, thank you for always believing in me. There are far too many of you to list individually, but please know that I have learned from every one of you.

Thank you to all the great companies that have served as the model for how businesses can successfully use social media and, for the purposes of this book, specifically, Facebook. You have paved the way and set the gold standards. Keep being innovative and not scared to take a little risk on finding new ways to connect with your prospects, customers, and fans.

Most of all, thank YOU for picking out this book among the thousands of others vying for your attention. It is my hope that what follows is useful to YOU.

We Want to Hear from You!

As the reader of this book, *you* are our most important critic and commentator. We value your opinion and want to know what we're doing right, what we could do better, what areas you'd like to see us publish in, and any other words of wisdom you're willing to pass our way.

As an associate publisher for Que Publishing, I welcome your comments. You can email or write me directly to let me know what you did or didn't like about this book—as well as what we can do to make our books better.

Please note that I cannot help you with technical problems related to the topic of this book. We do have a User Services group, however, where I will forward specific technical questions related to the book.

When you write, please be sure to include this book's title and author as well as your name, email address, and phone number. I will carefully review your comments and share them with the author and editors who worked on the book.

Reader Services

Visit our website and register this book at www.informit.com/title/9780789743213 for convenient access to any updates, downloads, or errata that might be available for this book.

Introduction

You can't seem to escape it. It's everywhere. On the news. On business cards. On your mobile phone. What is "it"? "It" is Facebook and it is part of a suite of online tools that change the way we communicate, build relationships, connect with one another, market, and do business.

The more people embrace it, others love to hate it; Facebook continues to grow into not "just another social network" but, instead, a powerhouse company that commands influence.

Many people question the viability of using Facebook as a main form of communication, not only personally but also professionally. Companies, rightfully so, have many questions regarding security, privacy, and how a website where you can comment on what your friends are doing, upload pictures and videos, and become a fan of just about anything in the world can actually help them to move needles that are important to them.

Facebook has become popular with not only individuals, but an increasing number of companies as well. Why? Because Facebook provides a suite of features that allow companies to develop communities, humanize their brands, engage with their prospects and customers, and many other benefits.

This book is a deep dive into how Facebook can be leveraged by your company starting TODAY. This book is not just a Facebook-is-cool-and-you-should-join type book. This book provides you with actionable information that you can begin implementing into your business. It gives you the ammunition you need to convince your boss, your board, your IT team, or your employees why they should be investing time and money on "just another social network."

This book addresses these concepts. We start with a brief overview of Facebook's history and move on from there to chat about the basics of getting around on the site, establishing a corporate presence, extending Facebook even deeper into the interwebs, Facebook Advertising, Facebook Apps, privacy concerns, and community development in Facebook. You work through designing a marketing plan geared directly for Facebook and understand why and how it will be different than any other marketing plan you put together. You then take a look at some of those individuals and companies who are best in class for their contribution to the Facebook community. You can extrapolate some of the concepts that they use, break them down, and discover the resources that you can then use for yourself or your company. This book finishes with where Facebook is going next. You take a look at this from both the macro and micro levels because you need to understand and attempt to predict both in the coming months and years of Facebook.

With that, understand that Facebook is growing and changing at such a fast pace that by the time you get your hands on this book, there will probably be another two dozen changes. Right up to the book going to press changes to the entire manuscript were made to keep it as current as possible.

With that said, buckle your seat belts, return and secure your tray tables and chairs to their full and upright position, and let's take a ride through Facebook with stops along the way to help you find practical business application uses for it.

Who Should Buy This Book

Simply put: This book is designed for professionals who want to understand how Facebook can be integrated into their business. This includes anyone from the CEO to the CMO to PR, communications, and marketing. Besides gaining an understanding of how you can use Facebook within your business, you can also gain an understanding of how YOU can use Facebook professionally as part of your own personal/professional branding.

How This Book Is Organized

Facebook Marketing is organized into 11 chapters.

Chapter 1, "From Dorm Room to Boardroom: The Growth of Social Networks," takes you from the beginning of Facebook in the founders' dorm rooms at Harvard University all the way to their corporate headquarters in San Francisco, California. This chapter provides an introduction to the phenomenon known as Facebook including major milestones such as opening the platform to everyone, going mainstream, and the major growth data points.

Chapter 2, "Getting Around Facebook: The Basics," deals with getting you around Facebook by taking a stroll through the basics. This includes a summary and detailed description of the basic profile options, notes, photos, videos, comments, likes, friends lists, Facebook Chat, and many other features. This chapter provides you with a foundation for going deeper into the platform and understanding how it can be integrated into your business.

In Chapter 3, "Establishing a Corporate Presence," you explore establishing a corporate presence including a deep dive into Facebook Pages and Groups. You gain an understanding of how to set up each of these features for your business, how they can be used, and which ones you should select based on your needs.

Chapter 4, "Extending Facebook into the Interwebs: The Power and Reach of Facebook Connect," breaks out of the framework of Facebook and discusses extending Facebook into the interwebs through the use of tools such as Facebook Connect. You learn how this major feature has been integrated into websites and how you can use it for your needs.

In Chapter 5, "Facebook Advertising: How and Why You Should Be Using It," you learn about the Facebook advertising platform and why you should use it. You learn about creating an ad, setting a budget, selecting cost-per-click (CPC) or cost-per-impressions (CPM), discovering your target audience, and using Facebook Insights (analytics).

To gain a full experience while using Facebook, you need to extend its capabilities with Facebook Apps. In Chapter 6, "Extending the Experience with Facebook Apps," I discuss plug-ins such as Flickr, Delicious, StumbleUpon, and several other applications that can help you to connect with your prospects, customers, and fans.

One of the most addressed issues throughout Facebook's history has been privacy. Chapter 7, "Addressing Privacy Concerns," reviews the changes of Facebook's privacy policy, whether you should have a personal AND professional Facebook account or if you need a single profile, and several other issues as it deals with your privacy, your customers' privacy, and the privacy of your company.

By the time you make it to Chapter 8, "Developing a Facebook Marketing Strategy," you will have developed a deeper understanding of Facebook and how you can use it as another part of your marketing toolbox. Chapter 8 helps you to pull all these tools together to develop a Facebook marketing strategy.

With all the described options, you learn that one of the best uses of Facebook for your business is through the development of communities. But how do you pull all this together? Chapter 9, "Using Facebook to Develop Communities," teaches you how you can use Facebook to develop communities.

Because you're not the first company to jump into Facebook, Chapter 10, "Best in Class," shows you some of the Best in Class companies that have fully utilized Facebook to build communities, engage with their audiences, and become more social. Some of these companies and people are those you already know: Coca-Cola, Microsoft Office, President Barack Obama, and many more.

To finish, Chapter 11, "Shaking the Crystal Ball: What's Next for Facebook," shakes the crystal ball and tries to guesstimate what's next for Facebook. This is your sandbox to play in to see if you can figure out where Facebook goes from here. Place your bets and let 'em ride!

Tips, Tricks, & Hacks

 Tip

Tips, tricks, and hacks are designed to point out features to help your experience with Facebook be smoother, more enjoyable, and more productive. As with the early days in school in math class, you'll have to learn some of the hard ways first and then we'll teach you quick tips, tricks, and hacks to help you.

From Dorm Room to Boardroom: The Growth of Social Networks

Over the past several years, social networks have become increasingly popular as they made their way into mainstream society mainly due to the ability to communicate in both real-time and asynchronously with a wide group of people. It is important to remember that the ability to use the Internet to communicate with a diverse and worldwide audience is not new and cannot be attributed solely to tools such as MySpace, Facebook, and Twitter. The ability to connect instantaneously with people from all around the world has been available to us since Prodigy decided to allow people to set up user groups around topics that interested them.

This paved the way to the creation of forum boards, user groups, chat rooms, IRC, instant messaging, and eventually, social networks as we know them today.

Nowadays these social networks come in all different shapes, sizes, and specialties. Do you love taking photos? Hop on Flickr. Want to communicate in short bursts of messages in real time. Head over to Twitter. A sucker for video? There's a service *a few* people have heard of called YouTube. Want something a little more specialized? How about a niche community encouraging members to stay fit? There's Twit2Fit that is run on the Ning social networking platform. Now, you want to track your workouts from getting back into shape, thanks in part to the support you get on Twit2Fit? Yep, there's a social network for that, too. You see, there is a social network for just about every broad and specific subject you could possibly want. Of course, some are more mainstream and "sticky" than others; therefore, there's more engagement and sharing by the community, and more iterating of the platform by the founding company. To understand just how many platforms there are and how many different communications verticals they span, Brian Solis and Jesse Stay created the Conversation Prism, shown in Figure 1.1.

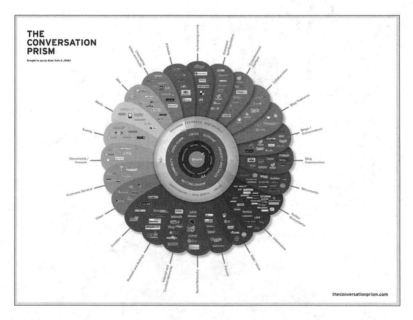

Figure 1.1   The Conversation Prism, created by Brian Solis and Jesse Stay, provides a visual representation of the social web. For more, visit theconversationprism.com.

These tools enable a single person to develop a personal brand that can compete with household consumer brands. Through the development of these personal brands, social networks, and blogs allow people to now be in control of *what* news others see. These social networks allow for the management of your online reputation. Besides these benefits, they create the ability for one person to use a platform to talk to thousands of people simply by hitting the Enter key. Social networks enable regular, normal, run-of-the-mill individuals, to become influencers and trusted resources to their communities. Yes, now YOU can develop your own personal communities. These communities can have a direct impact on your ability to build your business successfully by interacting with your prospects and customers online and building a strong fan base.

Social networks and blogs allow a wine store owner to connect with his community and help to grow his business from $4 million per year to over $60 million per year in revenue. These tools have helped a guy from north of Boston to develop such a strong community that they helped catapult a book he wrote onto the *New York Times* Bestsellers list only two days after the book was on store shelves. But, these tools have not only been beneficial to individuals. They have also helped some of the largest companies in the world reach out and start connecting with their customers on a one-to-one basis.

Businesses have greatly benefited from turning to social networks and integrating them as part of their marketing, communications, and customer service strategies. Using social networks has allowed businesses that embrace these tools to "humanize themselves." What do I mean by the term *humanize*?

For decades, companies have continued to grow through their ability to properly manage their brand by successfully marketing logos, catch phrases, slogans, and tag lines, all of which help to develop brand recognition. These companies became known by our ability to recognize their logos and get their jingles stuck in our heads, or the catchy tag line at the end of every commercial. At the same time, these same companies, in an effort to improve their bottom line, routinely looked at implementing systems and processes that automated as much as possible. Need to talk to customer service? Sure, there is a number to call. But, first, you're going to have to hit 1. Then 2. Type your account number. Type it again because you screwed up the first time. Say your last name. Now you're finally transferred to a human but because you hit 2 instead of 3 during the second step, you were sent to the wrong department. Now you have to be transferred elsewhere where you have to repeat all the information that you just inputted.

It's barriers like these that, while beneficial to the corporation, prevent them from highlighting the humans and personalities that help the corporation to function on a daily basis. Social networks help to change this. Humans can showcase the individual personalities that help to make them who they are. Companies can now cut out the phone trees and instantaneously interact with a single customer who is having an issue, which, to the customer, is one of the most serious things going on in his life at the very moment.

Besides just being active on social networks, these tools also enable businesses to, as Chris Brogan describes it, "grow bigger ears." You see, at any given moment, there are multiple conversations taking place about you, your brand, your products or services, your competition, and your industry. Imagine if you could monitor all this chatter in real time and had the ability to quickly respond? That would be valuable to you as a business, right? Hint: You want to be nodding your head up and down as fast as possible. If you're not, then put this book down, run head first into the wall, and start over again.

By way of the amount of data that users pour into these social networks on a daily basis, they allow us to monitor all those conversations with listening tools. These listening tools can alert us to any mentions of anything that is of interest to us. Someone bashes you on a blog post? The software service your company sells crashes for a user during a big presentation so he complains online? Your competition announces a major restructuring, product, or financial news? Yep, all these situations and much more can be monitored. In fact, these tools, because of their real-time nature, routinely provide information faster than Google can index it and quicker than news organizations can mobilize to broadcast.

Social networks have helped to grow businesses, elevate normal people to web celebrities, bring celebrities down to a human level, launch music careers, change national sentiment toward entire industries and assist in building and growing a community so strong that it helped to elect the 44th President of the United States of America.

One of the fastest growing and most popular social networks ever to be launched has been Facebook. With over 400 million users who generate billions of pieces of content, the social network has a larger population than most countries. When you first join Facebook, you immediately understand how it can be used to connect with family and friends. However, many people find themselves questioning the viability of using Facebook as a main form of communications professionally. Companies, rightfully so, have many questions regarding security, privacy, and how a website where you can comment on what your friends are doing, upload pictures, videos, and become a fan of just about anything in the world can actually help them to move needles that are important to them.

Throughout this book, I will tackle these very issues and help show you, both strategically and tactically, how Facebook can be used within your business. But first, let's start by exploring how a little social network that was created in a dorm room has become the behemoth that it is today.

About Marc Zuckerberg

Mark Zuckerberg (shown in Figure 1.2) was born on May 14, 1984 and was raised in Dobbs Ferry, NY. Though it would be a few years before Zuckerberg would create the top social network in the world, he began coding at an early age while he was in middle school. Zuckerberg attended Phillips Exeter Academy where he devised Synapse, a music player that leveraged artificial intelligence to learn users' listening habits. The technology that Zuckerberg created was so intriguing that it brought both Microsoft and AOL calling as both corporations tried recruiting Zuckerberg before he decided to attend Harvard University. But, that was not the only project keeping Zuckerberg busy while he attended Phillips Exeter Academy. Zuckerberg also built a version of the popular game, Risk, in addition to a program to help improve communications within his father's office. After Phillips Exeter Academy, Zuckerberg moved on to Harvard where he majored in computer science.

Figure 1.2   Mark Zuckerberg, Cofounder, CEO, and President of Facebook.

The Early Days

What would become the world's most popular social network only a few short years after its launch all started in February 2004 when Mark Zuckerberg launched "The Facebook," originally located at thefacebook.com (see Figure 1.3). Before becoming the richest person in the world under 25, Mark Zuckerberg was a sophomore at Harvard University when he developed The Facebook.

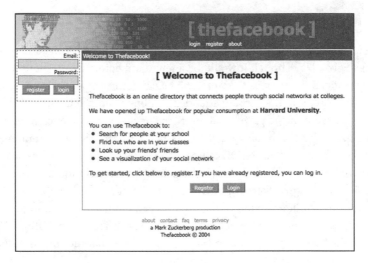

Figure 1.3   The original login screen to TheFacebook.com that launched on February 4, 2004 for Harvard University students only.

The Facebook came about after, during the previous semester, Zuckerberg created a Harvard version of a popular rating website "HOT or NOT." Zuckerberg called it Facemash, and it was intended to allow students at Harvard University to compare other students based on their online dorm Facebooks.

At the time that Zuckerberg was creating Facemash, HOT or NOT, as shown in Figure 1.4, was a popular rating site, founded in October 2000 by James Hong and Jim Young, that allowed users to vote whether pictures of people that were submitted to the site were HOT or NOT. As the HOT or NOT website describes

> HOT or NOT is the original place to rate, date, and hook up with single people 18–34. With millions rated using HOT or NOT's proprietary "RATE" feature, HOT or NOT is the official home of hotness...users can "MEET" other members through HOT or NOT's exclusive DoubleMatch™ dating engine. HOT or NOT also offers other fun options such as real-time chat, virtual flowers and gifts, and HOTLists™, which let members share their passions through personal selections of over 220,000 pictures of bands, movies, sports, TV shows, products, and hobbies.

At its height, HOT or NOT raked in an annual revenue approximated at $5 million with net profits of $2 million. Whether, at the time, HOT or NOT had already hit this success, and if they had, if Zuckerberg had known about it, the service was still very popular among college students. Therefore, it is no surprise that Zuckerberg saw an opportunity to create a private, internal network similar to the popular rating service, reserved only for Harvard students. Also, the basic tenets of the service

Figure 1.4   One of the original landing pages for HotorNot.com, which, at the height of its growth, would bring in annual revenue of approximately $5 million.

aren't features that would be hard for someone who had been coding their entire life to create.

The Facemash site launched on October 28, 2003 but was shut down by Harvard administration officials only a few days later because, to gain access to the pictures, Zuckerberg had hacked Harvard's computer network and copied over each of the nine residential houses' databases of ID photos. So, how did a HOT or NOT knockoff eventually iterate to become the world's largest and most popular social network to date?

It all started when Mark Zuckerberg added the site to the Kirkland House email list, which, at the time, was only approximately 300 people in total. However, from that single email, and Zuckerberg sharing his latest creation with a few friends, thefacebook.com spread so quickly that within the first month of its launch more than half of the undergraduates at Harvard during spring 2004 had signed up.

The Teenage Years

The Facebook was launched and, at first, was available only to Harvard University students. In March 2004, only one month after its initial launch, Zuckerberg expanded access to Stanford, Yale, and Columbia. Then Zuckerberg quickly expanded access to all Ivy League universities, then next to Boston area universities and colleges, and then across the United States and Canada. Although nothing specifically points to the geographic location of Harvard University as one of the reasons for the early explosive growth, it could be argued that it had a big effect. In the greater Boston area, there are well over 100 colleges and universities. The Northeast has the largest concentration of colleges and universities in the country. This helped Zuckerberg spread the social network quickly as it created demand for access as friends from different schools chatted with one another.

During its initial growth spurt at Harvard, Zuckerberg brought on Eduardo Saverin, Dustin Moskovitz, Andrew McCllum, and Chris Hughes to help with programming, graphic design, promotion, and other related tasks. The Facebook would later incorporate as a business during the summer of 2004. In June 2004, only 4 months after the platform's inception, Facebook would receive its first investment totaling $500,000 from Peter Thiel, cofounder of PayPal. For The Facebook to continue its Cinderella story, it would be necessary for the company to be located at the epicenter of technology, Silicon Valley. The Facebook moved operations out of the dorm rooms at Harvard and out to Palo Alto, California.

In 2005, The Facebook purchased facebook.com for $200,000 and dropped "The" from its name. Later that year, in September 2005, approximately a year and one-half after the initial launch, Facebook opened its network to high schools. It would be another year, in September 2006, that Facebook would completely open the network to anyone older than 13 with a valid email address.

During this time, Facebook continued to receive injections of cash to help it scale its operations to accommodate for the increase in demand from its users. In 2005, Facebook received venture capital funding from Accel Partners to the tune of $12.7 million. Facebook would receive another injection from Greylock Partners totaling $27.5 million in 2006.

To help Facebook continue expanding into international markets, in October 2007, Facebook and Microsoft expanded an advertising deal that gave Microsoft a $240 million equity stake in the social network. As a main pillar of Facebook's current revenue model, Facebook launched Facebook Ads a month later, in November 2007.

Coming into Adulthood

In January 2010, Mark Zuckerberg announced that Facebook had signed on its 400 millionth user. Consider that in September 2009, Zuckerberg announced the 300 millionth user, and not too long before that, in July 2009, he announced via the Facebook Blog that the network had surpassed its 250 millionth user since the site launched in February 2004. In only approximately 2 months, the social network had signed up an additional 50 million users. To put that number into even more perspective, consider that in April 2009, Zuckerberg had announced that Facebook had passed the 200 millionth user mark. The growth from 200 to 250 million users took Facebook approximately 90 days. The growth from 250 to 300 million users took roughly 60 days. That is a growth rate of approximately 833,000 users every day. To put that into even more perspective, that translates to approximately 35,000 users an hour or 578 every minute. Some estimates place the growth rate at approximately 750,000 new users per day.

Each time Facebook hit another growth milestone, it did it in record timing compared to previous accomplishments. Think Facebook is going away any time soon? Consider the following chronological growth patterns:

- February 2004: Facebook launches

- December 2004: Facebook reaches **1 million** active users.

- December 2005: Facebook reaches **5.5 million** active users.

- December 2006: Facebook reaches **12 million** active users.

- April 2007: Facebook reaches **20 million** active users.

- October 2007: Facebook reaches **50 million** active users.

- August 2008: Facebook reaches **100 million** active users.

- January 2009: Facebook reaches **150 million** active users.

- February 2009: Facebook reaches **175 million** active users.

- April 2009: Facebook reaches **200 million** active users.

- July 2009: Facebook reaches **250 million** active users.

- September 2009: Facebook reaches **300 million** active users.

From 2008 to June 2009, Facebook grew 157 percent, gaining an estimated 208 million visitors. As of June 2009, Facebook was receiving approximately 340 million unique visitors per month making it the fourth largest website in the world. The only websites with more monthly traffic are Google, Microsoft, and Yahoo. During the month of June 2009, it is estimated that Facebook grew by 24 million unique visitors as compared to May 2009. This type of traffic, and growing importance within the fabric of the interwebs, has led Facebook, according to paidContent.org, to pass Google as the top traffic driver to large sites.

To comprehend such astronomical numbers, let's look at Facebook at the 200 million active user mark. When Facebook hit the 200 million active users milestone, it produced a video about the race to 200 million people and provided these comparisons:

- It took 20,000 years for the world population to get to 200 million.

- It would take 46.5 years for 200 million babies to be born in the United States.

- If Facebook were a country, it would be the world's fifth most populous country, bigger than Brazil, Russia, and Japan.

Therefore, add in another 200 million users, at a current growth of 25 million new users per month or so, and it's not hard to realize why so much attention is being paid to Facebook. Will Facebook be the first social network to hit 1 billion active users? If their growth rate stabilizes and stays consistent at approximately 830,000 per day, Facebook is on pace to sign 1 billion active users by the start of 2012.

When you hear such large numbers of users flocking to any service, it always begs the question: Are they actually using the service or are they just signing up for an account that remains dormant?

For Facebook, its users are actively participating in the conversations and are spending a lot of their time doing so. Brian Solis (briansolis.com), a thought leader, prolific blogger, speaker, and author, dug up these stats:

- More than 5 billion minutes are spent on Facebook each day (worldwide).

- 30 million users update their statuses at least once each day.

- 8 million users "fan" Fan Pages each day.

- 120 million users log into their Facebook account each day.

- 1 billion photos are uploaded to Facebook each month.

- 10 million videos are uploaded to Facebook each month.

- 1 billion social objects are shared each week.

- 2.5 million events are created each week.

- 45 million active user groups exist on Facebook.

- 30 million users currently access Facebook through their mobile devices.

So why is everyone running to join Facebook? Facebook seemed to come of age at a time when simple and functional design wins out. Over the years, Facebook has continued to maintain a clean, organized user interface despite adding tons of new features. Facebook is similar to Google in that way. Besides being a superior search engine compared to Yahoo, MSN, and others, Google wins over users because it is simple and easy to use, yet is a powerful engine. Facebook represents the same for the social networking space.

Facebook provides an easy-to-understand interface, thus making it appeal to all ages. For the less tech savvy, it is manageable without a lot of help. Those that are tech savvy can take full advantage of the multitude of settings, options, and flexibility of the platform to share and engage.

It should come as no surprise that the largest growth age range for Facebook is between 35–55. This flies in the face of what many people believe is the stereotype user of a social network such as Facebook. But, it is no longer for only college students. That's so 2005. Facebook is now for your parents and your grandparents. It is for your colleagues and your supervisors. It's for individuals, celebrities, brands, products, services, musicians, and anyone else that finds it useful to fish where the fish are whether it's for friends, ex-lovers, business opportunities, fans, or constituents. Facebook is now mainstream and poised to continue its rapid growth rate.

To highlight Facebook's injection into mainstream, in January 2009, during the inauguration of the 44th President of the United States, Barack Obama, CNN Live and Facebook teamed up to provide real-time updates from Facebook's users in line with the live coverage by CNN. The result was a live video stream window side-by-side with a Facebook integration that displayed status updates, as shown in Figure 1.5, from all Facebook users regarding the Inauguration. It is estimated that 8,500 status updates per minute were captured during the Inauguration. After the massive success of this integration, Facebook would again make a similar partnership, but this time with the NBA. During the NBA All-Star game, Facebook provided a real-time stream of status updates about the 2009 NBA All-Star game. Facebook followed this up with a live stream integration during the 2009 Grammy's.

Figure 1.5   During President Obama's Inauguration speech, Facebook logged 8,500 status updates per minute. (Screenshot by David Orban.)

Such partnerships have proven successful for Facebook as it serves as a proving ground to those that are resistant to using the service. Certainly, there were probably viewers of CNN Live, the Grammy's, and the NBA All-Star game who are skeptical about the service or continued to think it was only for high school and college students. But having the integration in place with a network such as CNN, which is arguably the top news network, during one of the most important chapters of our nation's history to date, served as a milestone for the social network.

Facebook isn't only growing its user base at a blistering pace: It continues to build out its organization and gain market power. To accommodate this growth, during 2009, Facebook opened its new headquarters located in Palo Alto. During 2010, Facebook is poised to grow its internal team by adding a new office in Austin, Texas with an initial group of 300 team members. That is in addition to other smaller, satellite offices all over the country. No longer is Facebook working out of multiple rented office spaces, coffee shops, and bookstores.

With the rapid growth and popularity that Facebook continues to experience, there have been several estimated valuations of the company. Probably the best stat to look at is from a May 2009 investment from Digital Sky Technologies to the tune of $200 million. The investment deal between Digital Sky Technologies and Facebook was for preferred stock at a $10 billion valuation. With this intensive growth has also come fame and fortune for its founder, Mark Zuckerberg.

Zuckerberg is the youngest person to ever be named to the Forbes 400 list. In 2008, Forbes estimated Zuckerberg's net worth at approximately $1.5 billion, making him the 321st richest person in the United States.

Although Facebook has faced competition from other social networks such as Twitter, FriendFeed, MySpace, Flickr, and other smaller services, it seems as though it can't be stopped. In August 2009, Facebook acquired FriendFeed for, roughly, $50 million. This purchase came after approximately one year of FriendFeed continuing to grow its user base and implementing new features that left Facebook users begging for. As these new features were released, interestingly enough, they would appear on the Facebook platform not long after.

This is one of the marks of Facebook so far. When other services implement features that its platform currently does not support, usually, not too long afterward, we see the same services appear in Facebook. Most notably was the integration in February 2009, before its acquisition of FriendFeed, of the Likes feature that had become so popular among FriendFeed users. In September 2009, Facebook finally responded to demands from the users to implement a status-tagging feature to ping (alert) other users or Pages when they've been mentioned in a status update. Again, similar to the Likes feature from FriendFeed, this alert feature is a combination of @ replies in Twitter coupled with the tagging feature in Facebook Photos and Videos.

I opened my Facebook account after I graduated from college, though only by a couple months; I was not part of the initial surge of people who rushed to the service. Though it is interesting to see the fast growth of the 35+ group of users, I have spoken with many people who have told me stories about multiple generations of their families being on Facebook. I don't foresee my grandparents jumping on the service any time soon but think it would be interesting to receive a comment from them to a status or link I posted.

I know what you're thinking right now. First, you probably didn't realize that Facebook was that large. Don't worry—you're not alone. Almost every person I talk to doesn't believe me. But, now that you know, how can you jump in and get involved (or more involved)? Can you take the available features and turn Facebook into a successful tool for communicating with your prospects and customers? What about privacy?

All these questions and plenty more will be answered in the upcoming chapters. Along the way I explain the features and their basic functions, and then highlight how you can begin using them for your business. For those of you who like case studies and stories of success, don't worry, I have you covered. If you walk about after finishing this book and think "Oh, that was interesting" and never do anything with the information, then I failed to do my job. If, instead, you take this book, scribble throughout it, call a team meeting, grab a blank whiteboard, and start strategizing about how you're going to integrate Facebook (and other social networks) into the fold of your business, fantastic.

The most important thing is for you to keep an open mind as you flip the pages of this book. Understand the social networks, especially ones such as Facebook, *are* the new way to communicate and market your brand. You can either choose to embrace it or watch your competition pass you as they figure it out. For the non-believers who are reading this book, this is your call-to-action. Enough is enough. It's time to accept that social networks aren't going anywhere. For those of you who are already deeply engaged in social networks such as Facebook, I hope that I can shed light on some ideas and features that you haven't previously considered using.

Let's start this journey by going over some of the basics....

Getting Around Facebook: The Basics

If you're new to Facebook or just considering whether to join, this chapter can help you to get up and running quickly. As Facebook continues to grow, at the rate at which it's growing, at times it can be hard to keep up with all the updates it keeps pumping out, such as enhancements and new features. Although getting around Facebook isn't exactly hard, this chapter covers some of the basic tools and features.

If you're an experienced Facebook user, feel free to skim through this chapter or entirely skip it and go to the next chapter about establishing a corporate presence.

What you won't find in this chapter is an exact step-by-step process. Actually, you won't find that anywhere throughout this book. You want actionable and descriptive information that can help you immediately, not a step-by-step tutorial.

Getting Started

First of all, congrats! If you're considering whether to join, just joined, or if you are an experienced user, you're part of one of the fastest growing and largest social networks in history. There are millions of people who share your same interests, hobbies, career goals, and just about anything else you can think of. But, to find all these friends, networking opportunities, and groups, you have to know how and where to look. You also have to then take the time to actually invest into the building of your presence on Facebook.

With that said, let's get you up and running as quickly as possible so that you can start reaping all the wonderful benefits that Facebook has to offer.

To start, simply go to www.facebook.com. When the page loads, you notice a section for new users to sign up, as shown in Figure 2.1. Pop in your basic information, press Sign Up, and we're off to the races.

Figure 2.1   The Facebook landing page where you can either sign up for an account or log into your account.

After you register and log into Facebook for the first time, you need to do a few things immediately.

0-60 on Facebook in 11 Steps

1. Take a Few Minutes to Familiarize Yourself

This is either a new world you're stepping into or a social network you're determined to spend more time hanging out on. It has lots of features, as shown in

Figure 2.2—many of which we discuss. Click around; you won't break anything. (Well, hopefully you won't break anything.)

Figure 2.2   After you log into Facebook, you see the home page that serves as your dashboard to access many of the different features of your Facebook account.

2. Upload a Picture of Yourself

We want to see who you are. When someone searches for you, they're much more likely to engage and recognize you if they're greeted with a nice picture. When you do searches in Facebook, the search results provide you with only those people's pictures, names, and networks. Therefore it can be hard to identify people you're looking for if they don't have a picture uploaded, especially if it's a common name. For this reason, uploading a profile photo is a must. Besides, one of the reasons you're probably hanging out on Facebook, besides using it for your marketing needs, is to have meaningful personal relationships. Pictures help really well with that. On the marketing side, a photo helps to humanize your brand. It allows your prospects, customers, and fans to connect directly with you and know exactly who they are talking to.

Please don't post anything offensive. Facebook isn't the right place for offensive pictures, and Facebook actively polices the network. At a basic level, why would you even want to upload a picture that was offensive to a network that you don't control and in a world where everything you do becomes a permanent record?

Please post a picture of yourself that shows your personality. The most preferred type of photo to upload as your profile picture is a nice one of you by yourself, either a headshot or a full body picture. This allows the focus to be on you, and people don't have to guess which person you might be. Also, remember that the profile picture in search results and other areas of the network appear much smaller. If there are other people, animals, or objects in the photo, it will make it harder to distinguish what's going on and who's actually in the photo. But, if you prefer not to upload a photo of just yourself, have fun uploading an action shot, one of you with an animal or with your significant other/friend. Uploading group pictures as your profile picture should be a no-no, just because it will be near-impossible to see you in it, especially if someone has never seen a photo of you or met you before.

3. Fill Out Your Profile Completely

I know this seems like it will take forever, but this is one of the main ways that people can find you. It's the quickest way for me to get to know you when you accept my friendship request. Also, some of the ever-increasing applications that are created for Facebook can leverage some of this information to help keep contact lists up to date, such as on the iPhone, Palm Pre, and Android platforms.

Some of the information you have the option to enter and that you will be prompted to fill in, as shown in Figure 2.3, includes the following: sex, birthday, home town, relationship status, type of connections you want to establish, interests, favorite music, favorite TV shows, favorite movies, favorite books, quotations, a little information about yourself, contact information, and your education and work background.

Figure 2.3 The Info tab of your Facebook account that contains all the basic information you choose to share about yourself.

Now, you don't have to fill ALL this out and should fill out only questions that you feel comfortable with having posted. If you don't want to display your full contact info, that's understandable. If you prefer not to mention your political preference, don't. But, do take the time to share as much as you're comfortable with.

Tip

If you're a married woman who has changed her name, consider including your maiden name so that old friends and family can more easily find you. Remember, they might not know that you're married.

4. Start Finding Some Friends

The main way in which you connect with people on Facebook is through *friending* them. These people can be family, friends, colleagues, business partners, or people who want to connect for a variety of other reasons. There is no "right" number for the total number of friends you should have. You shouldn't be focused on the number. Be focused on finding interesting people, many of whom you already know, and connect with them as often as possible. Facebook provides a perfect platform for relationship development, personal and professional networking, and the ability to connect with old friends, family, and colleagues.

As Nick O'Neill of AllFacebook.com points out: "One of the biggest challenges on Facebook is the loss of new users that are not able to connect immediately with other members." With that said, you can find people to connect with on Facebook in a number of ways. The following are just a few of the ways, but if you use these, it can definitely help to get you up to speed.

If you use one of the more popular email services such as Gmail or Yahoo, head on over to the Friend Finder section, as shown in Figure 2.4, and pop in your email and password. (Don't worry; Facebook isn't selling it to some foreign country.) Facebook searches the people you communicate with via email and spits back a list of people it finds who are on Facebook. Easy cheesy.

As shown in Figure 2.5, you can upload your contact file if you use a work email service that pops through Outlook, iMail, Entourage, or another desktop email software. This can also be done through the Friend Finder section.

5. Import your AOL Instant Messenger (AIM) or Windows Live Buddies

Based on the educational and work information you input into your profile, Facebook creates saved searches that you can click on to run a search on everyone that you graduated high school or college with, for example. Alternatively, you can go directly to your profile and click on the name of your school or company to also run that search.

Figure 2.4   The Friend Finder section where you can enter your email information and Facebook will search your address book to find people who you communicate with who also have a Facebook account.

Figure 2.5   If you don't use one of the popular email services such as Gmail or Yahoo to manage your contacts or you prefer to keep your address book outside of email services, you can upload a contact file to the Friend Finder as well.

You can run an advanced search, found on the Friend Finder section (see Figure 2.6). This allows you to search by name, email, school name, or company.

From your profile, based on the amount of information you input, you can click any of the automatically hyperlinked items to run a saved search based on that topic. For example, if you enter that Jay-Z is one of your favorite musicians, you can click that name to produce a results page of everyone else who also added Jay-Z as one of their favorite artists (see Figure 2.7).

This is a great feature to help you connect with people who might be outside of your immediate network but who share similar interests with you. You can even find some of your friends who share the same interests with you that you didn't previously know about. Then it gives you another talking point the next time you get together.

Figure 2.6   Using the Advanced section of the Friend Finder you can search for friends, family, or colleagues by searching based on their email address, school, or company.

Figure 2.7   After you fill in your information on the Info tab, these choices become hyperlinked. You can then click those choices to run a search of other Facebook users who have also made the same choice, such as a favorite music artist.

Search—You can find your friends simply by searching their name (see Figure 2.8). If your friends have a common name, you might get a lot of results thrown back at you. You can use the My Networks filter or Profile Search tools to help ease the pain. As you run your searches, you can also see any conversations taking place around your friends where their names are used in status updates, links, and so on.

Running searches is the most manual of the processes but is the one you use the most after you run through the preceding steps.

As your friends begin to accept your friend requests, Facebook asks them to make friend suggestions to help you grow your network as shown in Figure 2.9. This can happen only in the beginning until Facebook senses that you have developed a strong network.

As you continue to grow your network Facebook provides you with friend suggestions based on mutual friends you may share, similar interests, and such. This can

Figure 2.8   The results section of running a search based on name.

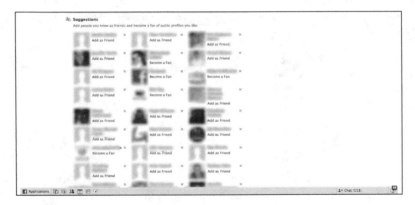

Figure 2.9   The friend suggestion tool in Facebook.

be a great way to connect with people who you might be following on other networks and through the previously mentioned methods, when you still haven't found each other.

As shown in Figure 2.10, I am not currently friends with Aaron Brazell (though I follow him on Twitter and love his blog), and Facebook sensed some reason to suggest that we connect. Upon looking at Aaron's profile, I can see that we share 91 mutual friends. Therefore, it makes sense that Aaron and I just haven't had the opportunity to run into each other before, but we share many of the same friends.

There are also add-in tools for Outlook, such as Xobni that searches the email address against the Facebook database as you go through emails and allows you to quickly and easily send friend requests (see Figure 2.11).

As you find friends, add a short personal message into the friend request. It makes it, well, more personal.

Figure 2.10   The Mutual Friends feature in Facebook for showing other users who you connect to through mutual friends but who are not yet connected directly.

Figure 2.11   Outlook plug-in Xobni searches the email addresses of those who you receive email from or send email to and matches with their Facebook profile directly within Outlook.

6. Upload More Photos

Uploading a profile photo or two just isn't enough. We want to learn more about you. We want to see more than just that headshot and the basic information you provided. One of the ways that you can do that is through creating albums and uploading photos to Facebook.

Go through and pick out a handful of your favorite photos and create your first photo albums on Facebook. Many people, including myself, go straight to people's photos as the quickest way to learn more about them. I like to see where you've been, you having fun with your family, joking around at the office, or anything else you're willing to share.

Facebook makes it easy to upload a lot of pictures at once by allowing you to browse your computer's hard-drive and select all or grab just a specific selection. Facebook also gives you the ability to upload directly from your phone; or if you're a Mac user, you can use iPhoto as well.

As you grow your list of friends, you can go back through and "tag" any friends of yours who appear in your photos, too (see Figure 2.12). Warning: This can become addictive.

Figure 2.12   The tagging feature within Facebook Photos.

7. Upload a Video or Two

Do you have a short video that you shot on vacation, during the holidays, or last Friday night when you were out with friends? Throw it up there. Because we might never have met in real life, uploading photos and videos is the way that I can connect with you and match your personality with the words that are on the screen.

Don't have any videos? Start creating 'em. Use a webcam, iSight (if you're a Mac owner), your phone, your digital camera, or Flip camera and start capturing some of the mayhem that you're causing. Just like photos, you can tag your friends in videos as well.

As a piece of advice, try to keep the video under 3–5 minutes. Everyone is really busy and the longer you make the video, the less likely people are to watch it, share it, or maybe even blog about it. Keep it short and fun!

8. Send Your First Status Using the Publisher Tool

Updating your status is how we know what you're up to, what you're thinking, and how you'll share anything you find interesting such as links, photos, videos, and a whole lot more depending on what applications you install. You certainly don't need to update your status 487 times per day. A few times per day would be perfect. (See Figure 2.13 for an example.)

Figure 2.13   The Publisher Tool within Facebook—your primary communications tool to share information.

Updating your status can help you to stay top-of-mind with friends as your status jumps into the News Feed giving your friends the chance to leave comments and like or share the stuff you're putting in.

9. Download a Facebook Mobile Application

Are you part of the ever increasing population that's using a smartphone such as an iPhone, a BlackBerry, a Palm Pre, or an Android-platform device? If so, grab the Facebook app made for your device. Alternatively, you can use the mobile version of Facebook by heading over to m.facebook.com. This allows you to easily add new content such as photos and videos, update your status, see what you're friends are up to, and access a number of other features while you're on-the-go. If it weren't for the mobile app, my Facebook usage would be much lower than what it is. It allows me to constantly produce content and share what I'm up to, even if I am away from my laptop or not near an Internet connection.

10. Start Interacting with Your Friends

Facebook allows you this great opportunity to connect with friends, colleagues, and people you meet. Take advantage of it. Cruise around and look at the photos and videos your friends upload. Check out some links your friends share. Leave a comment or two; share something they've said or "Like" a few things. But, a word of caution, please don't "own" your friends Facebook accounts. There is no need to comment or like everything that they post. This will not only become annoying but also can start to seem disingenuous. Comment on a couple items per day and you'll be on the road to success.

11. Have Fun and Explore!

The most important thing you can do is try to have fun. If you're not having fun, you're less likely to use it. That's definitely not what any of us want to happen. You're reading this book to find how you can leverage Facebook better personally and professionally. If you don't have fun with the basic steps, everything that comes after will make you want to run around with scissors.

Take some time, get used to how things work around Facebook, and have fun. It can eat up a lot of your time if you let it, but that's okay. Remember that this is all about making connections, interacting, and building or strengthening trust. The only way any of that can happen is if you put in time, have fun, and are genuine throughout the entire process. Besides, it's not really "eating up your time" as much as it is making an investment in your future by allowing you a way to develop personal and professional relationships with others.

Although these 11 steps certainly don't cover everything that you will find yourself doing when you first sign up, it can definitely have you feeling right at home sooner than later.

Now that we have your profile filled out, a few pictures, maybe a video, and you're starting to get friend requests, we should go over a few of the basic features and tools.

Home Page Feed

When you first log into Facebook, you are directed to the home page, as shown in Figure 2.14. This page can be accessed at any time by clicking Home on the top toolbar. The home page is your real-time news feed of what your friends share on Facebook. All their status updates and anything they choose to share such as photos, videos, new applications, and so on appear here.

If the news stream is overwhelming, you can filter it down based on the networks you belong to and the type of update it is (see Figure 2.15). Therefore, if you wanted to see only all new pictures that have been uploaded, you can choose the Photos option on the left toolbar to filter out everything else except for newly uploaded photos.

Besides the news stream running down the center of the page, you also notice some other widgets along the right sidebar. Facebook displays any requests that are made of you such as friend requests, friend detail requests, event invitations, page invitations, or anything else where you need to take action.

Figure 2.14 The home page showing the news feed and other features in the right sidebar.

Figure 2.15 Using the filters for the news feed on the home page.

Below the requests widget, Facebook displays a single friend or Page suggestion at a time. You can either take action to friend or fan them or you can "x" out that suggestion to replace it with another. Next up are highlights of pictures that your friends are uploading and upcoming events that you can choose to attend.

The home page is valuable because it serves as your dashboard into Facebook. If you don't have a lot of time on a given day, the home page allows you to jump in quickly, see what's going on, maybe make a few comments, accept a couple friend requests, wish a friend Happy Birthday, and then get out.

When the news feed was first introduced, it was met with a lot of resistance. It had been nicknamed a "stalker feed" because it posts any changes to your profile to the news feed for all to see. Change your relationship status before remembering to tell your now ex-significant other? Yup, everyone else will see before he or she knows. Decide you want to want to change your favorite movies? You got it; it will post to the news feed. Several groups had been created that are against the news feed, as shown in Figure 2.16, but Facebook kept it in place.

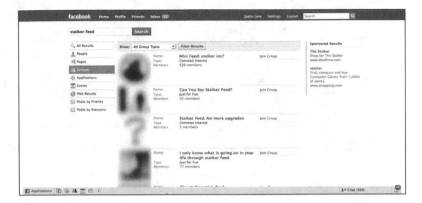

Figure 2.16 Some of the groups that are still available bashing the news feed and renaming it a "stalker feed."

However, as time continued and Facebook continued to enhance the news feed by adding a real-time environment, commenting, and likes, people seemed to become more comfortable. Besides these enhancements, Facebook also tweaked the available privacy settings, so users could decide what they were comfortable with sharing.

With the introduction of these enhancements, the news feed began to win over its critics. Now, instead of just being a one-way push of your changes within the service, it now displays everything that you've chosen to share through the Publisher tool or automatic updates. It has also given users the ability to jump in and comment or "like," in real-time, what their friends are posting. The home page/news feed has created more of a real-time two-way communications channel outside of Facebook Chat, on the platform, thus increasing user engagement with one another and with the tool.

Comments and Likes

As mentioned, one of the enhancements that Facebook made was the adoption of a FriendFeed feature that allows users to comment on or "like" what others are posting. This increased engagement between users because previously your only option was to actually comment on the other person's Wall. Although you could choose the Wall-to-Wall option to view the threaded conversation, it still wasn't as good as the commenting feature is.

One of the nice features of commenting and likes is the notification, if you have it activated, when others jump in and comment on or like that particular update. This allows for that back-and-forth communications channel that we've been talking about.

If you don't have a comment to leave but found the update interesting, you can choose to simply "like" the update, which essentially means giving it a thumbs up.

One of the features that is missing since Facebook introduced this enhancement is a reporting tool that allows you to view all updates that you have commented on or liked. However, with Facebook's acquisition of FriendFeed, I'm sure this will be a feature that will soon be available, if it's not already available by the time you're reading this book.

Publisher Tool

When you click the Profile tab at the top of your window, you'll be brought to YOUR profile. You'll immediately notice this box with a question inside simply asking: What's on your mind? This is called the Publisher tool within Facebook, and it serves as your main portal to sharing information with your network (see Figure 2.17).

Figure 2.17   Using the Publisher tool to send a status update that will be dropped into the general news feed based on my preferences.

The Publisher tool initially started out as a field to simply update your status. But as the platform grew, Facebook updated it to support the sharing of videos, photos, events, smart links, and more options. (Facebook automatically scans a link to pull a title, description, and photo from the site you're sharing, as shown in Figure 2.18.)

Figure 2.18 Adding a link into the Publisher tool. This example shows a YouTube video that Facebook detected and automatically pulled in. The video can then be played directly within the status update.

At the end of June 2009, Facebook made another enhancement to the Publisher tool by allowing users to control the privacy settings around status updates made through the tool (see Figure 2.19). Previous to this enhancement any status you posted would be public to everyone. But, with the new updates, you now have a choice to make your status updates visible by everyone, your network and friends, friends of friends, only friends, or a customized list.

Figure 2.19 Some of the many privacy settings that you can control that dictate the level of sharing and access to your profile or individual settings within your profile.

Why did Facebook change these privacy settings? According to a Facebook blog post regarding this update: "You may have some posts you want to share with a wide audience, such as whom you voted for or how great the weather is today. Other times you may have more personal updates like your new phone number or an invitation to join you at your favorite restaurant for dinner that are meant for only close or nearby friends."

To control these privacy options, roll over the Settings link at the top of your window, choose Privacy Settings, and select the Profile option. You notice the options to control your status settings about halfway down. We address privacy issues in greater detail in Chapter 7, "Addressing Privacy Concerns," but the update to the Publisher tool was definitely one of biggest steps Facebook made into giving users more privacy controls.

Photos

The photo feature within Facebook is probably the platform's most-used feature. More than 1 billion photos are uploaded and shared on Facebook every month. This makes Facebook the top photo-sharing site in the world.

So what is it that makes everyone go so crazy over photos? It is probably the ease with which you can upload them. In a few clicks you can gain access to your entire photo library on your hard-drive, and you can begin uploading everything into customized photo albums that you have defined within Facebook. Each photo album can hold only 200 photos, which is far better than the previous limit of approximately 70. But, if you just came back from vacation and have a few hundred pictures that you want to upload, you need to create several albums.

When you upload photos to Facebook, you have the option of publishing a preview of these pictures to your Wall, which will also drop them into the news stream. This is a great way to alert your network that you have uploaded new photos you want them to check out.

In addition to having the ability to upload and share pictures, Facebook allows you to tag your friends in the pictures that you upload. To use the tag feature, they must be a Facebook user and a friend of yours. When you tag someone, it automatically sends them a notice that they've been tagged in a photo and, depending on their privacy settings, it posts that photo onto their Wall and into the View Photos of Me area directly below their profile picture (see Figure 2.20).

The photo feature really took off with college and high school students who typically carry digital cameras or camera-phones everywhere they go.

There have definitely been privacy concerns raised over the tagging of photos, which we discuss more in Chapter 7. Suffice it to say though, you shouldn't be uploading anything to Facebook that you're nervous about ANYONE else seeing, whether or not they're your friend on the network.

Figure 2.20   The View Photos of Me feature where all tagged pictures of you are aggregated.

Videos

Similar to the photo feature, Facebook allows you to upload, share, and tag videos. If you tag yourself or are tagged in a video, it appears in the View Videos of Me section right below your profile picture, as shown in Figure 2.21.

Figure 2.21   The View Videos of Me feature that is similar to the "View Photos of Me" feature.

Facebook provides you the option of uploading a video from your hard drive or another source that you can browse out to, emailing a mobile video using a custom email address, or recording directly into Facebook (see Figure 2.22). Although videos are not as popular as photos, more than 10 million videos upload to Facebook each month.

One of the reasons videos probably aren't as popular is that we're just starting to see the introduction of phones that can capture and upload video. However, with the

Figure 2.22   The Videos feature in Facebook where you can either upload a video or record a video directly into Facebook.

introduction of digital cameras that can capture quality video and devices such as the Flip, I think we'll see the use of video on Facebook continue to increase.

With Apple's release of the iPhone 3GS in July 2009, which introduced the ability to capture and upload video on the iPhone, YouTube reported that in the first six days of the release, it saw an increase in video uploads of 400 percent. Although similar numbers aren't available for Facebook, I believe we'll continue to see the number of videos uploaded to Facebook continue to rise.

Another reason for the slower growth of videos is that Facebook doesn't allow you to upload videos from resources such as TubeMogul, which allow you to upload the video once and push it out to multiple video networks. So, what that means is that I can upload a video to TubeMogul and push it out to YouTube, Viddler, Blip.tv, Vimeo, and 20 other video networks at once. But, to get it onto Facebook, I then have to log into the service and spend time uploading it there as well. The more steps anyone has to take to publish content, the less likely she is to do it. But, I'd suggest taking that extra time because you have an established community on Facebook that might not also be following you on these other video sharing services. Therefore, if you don't upload your video to Facebook, you might miss out on an opportunity to connect with your community.

Pages and Groups

Facebook provides you the option to build, find, and be part of communities built around topics, products, brands, celebrities, and just about anything else you can think of. Do a search for some of your favorite hobbies, bands, or companies. If they have a presence on Facebook, consider becoming a *fan*. Not only will you be joining a community of like-minded folks who you can interact with in a variety of ways, but it'll also be added to your profile so that other people can see where you like to hang out on Facebook and what you're interested in.

In Chapter 3, "Establishing a Corporate Presence," we discuss how YOU can create a successful Page or Group for your company, service, or product including how to properly gain exposure, cultivate the community, and leverage your fans to help spread your message.

Notes

You'll notice one of the available default tabs for your profile is a feature called *Notes*. Facebook describes this feature as "With Facebook Notes, you can share your life with your friends through written entries. You can tag your friends in notes, and they can leave comments." This might seem similar to the blog feature in MySpace that a lot of people used but that never quite resonated the way the MySpace team intended.

Facebook Notes are used by some people as a blogging platform, though it isn't recommend because there are much better, professional platforms out there such as WordPress, MoveableType, and TypePad. Others use it to post stories about friends that they can then tag or things that they find that are interesting. However, the majority of users I see using the application use Notes as a means of importing their blog via RSS (see Figure 2.23).

Figure 2.23 The Notes feature that is most commonly used to pull in the RSS feed of a blog external to Facebook.

Notes allow you to add in the RSS feed (a web feed format used to publish new blog posts) from your external blog that it will then ping, suck in, and post to your Wall whenever you publish a new post. Facebook users can comment on, share, and subscribe to these posts (er, notes) from within Facebook. It is one of the simplest ways of pulling in your RSS feed and is a great way to extend the reach of your blog.

Facebook Chat

When Facebook originally launched, it was during a time when instant messaging was becoming a primary communications tool for many high school and college students. Facebook users would stop by Facebook to post a status update, upload a few photos, or check in on their friends, but they still did the bulk of their communicating using other tools such as AIM, Yahoo IM, Google Talk, and so on.

Although Facebook didn't face any competition from these services as far as feature offerings, Facebook still wants to keep users on its page as long as possible. The longer users stay on the Facebook site, the more likely they are to share, take a few more minutes to upload that batch of photos, or search for a few more friends.

With that in mind, Facebook launched Facebook Chat, its instant messaging tool. Facebook Chat allows you to instantly message and chat with any of your friends who are logged into Facebook. From the chat window, which resides at the bottom of the window (see Figure 2.24), you can launch into that user's profile.

Figure 2.24   Facebook Chat used within Facebook. You can also use Facebook Chat in IM aggregator services such as Adium.

As Facebook Chat has continued to grow, several instant messaging applications have been created to help users consolidate their various IM services into one tool (such as Adium, Jabber, and Meebo).

Search

As Facebook gained more and more users, it became clear that the standard search feature would not be enough. Originally Facebook Search allowed you to search only for people, Groups, or Pages based on name only. Any of the information that was entered in status updates, for example, was not searchable. This was the largest edge that Twitter had over Facebook.

With Twitter Search (http://search.twitter.com), users can search the conversations taking place on the network in real time. Users can grab customized RSS feeds based on the search criteria, and then those can be sucked into a feed reader such as Google Reader (www.google.com/reader). For a long time, Facebook took criticism because it didn't have a more robust search engine, especially because Facebook has hundred of millions of users compared to tens of millions using Twitter.

In June 2009, Facebook announced that it was experimenting with an enhanced search feature to help users mine through the tons of information that pumps into the platform on a daily basis. Approximately 2 months later, Facebook released the new search feature. According to a Mashable article posted shortly after the release, "The new search will crawl the last 30 days of news feed activity—specifically status updates, photos, links, videos and notes from your friends' Facebook profiles and the pages of which you are a Fan. It will also crawl any public profiles and status updates" (see Figure 2.25).

Figure 2.25   The Search feature used to search for mentions of President Obama.

This was a major announcement by Facebook and one that pushed the social network even further ahead of its competition. With the release of the new search feature, Facebook is now directly challenging Twitter, which has become extremely popular at conferences, sporting events, and other public events because of the ability to use a hashtag (#) that is searchable to show the aggregated conversations taking place. It's reasonable to believe that Facebook would be readying something similar if it really is gunning directly for Twitter Search with this feature.

Either way, Facebook Search is a useful feature to search through all the data that your community is sharing on the network every day.

Friends Tab

The Friends tab allows you to segment your friends into different lists, as shown in Figure 2.26. This is helpful especially when you get past having a handful of friends. You can classify your friends into any list as you determine in addition to some of the basic lists/searches that Facebook already has set up for you. This is useful especially with the enhanced privacy features for status updates and the sharing of information. If you've created segmented lists, you can choose to share certain updates or information only with a particular list. That means that your college buddies don't have to see the industry news that you want to share with your professional contacts, if you don't want them to.

Figure 2.26 The Friends tab where you can create different lists to enable you to filter your friends quickly.

One of the really cool features of the Friends tab is the Phonebook option. Because Facebook asks you to input your phone number on the Info tab of your profile, you can roll that up into a useable phonebook of your contacts. I have found that approximately 30 percent of my friends actually input their phone number. For a large percentage of those people, I didn't have their phone number previously. This becomes useful if you're going to a conference or meeting and forget to ask someone who you want to meet up with for his phone number. If you're friends with him on Facebook and he stored his number, you can grab it easily. The Facebook app made for the iPhone allows you to sync that information up with your standard address book. If you're a Pre user, Pre has the ability to access the Facebook Phone Book as it syncs up with your other address books on services such as Google, your desktop app, and so on.

Inbox Tab

Facebook, like many other social networks, has its own internal email system. This can be accessed via the Inbox tab at the top of your screen. From there, you can send Facebook email to any one of your friends (see Figure 2.27). Facebook also allows you to attach links, photos, videos, or other application updates (depending on the actual application) similar to the Publisher Tool.

Figure 2.27   The Facebook Inbox where users can email each other and Groups or Pages administrators can send messages to their communities.

The Facebook Inbox is one of the features that has not really been updated by Facebook in some time. Though they are currently working on updates that are supposed to revolutionize the way that the email system works.

Settings Tab

The Settings tab is your landing area to control everything to do with your Facebook account (see Figure 2.28). From the Settings area you can control your account, privacy, and application settings. You can choose what types of notifications you want to receive and how you want to receive them. You can select what you want to be shared from your profile and with whom. There are a ton of settings under this area, and you should take some time tweaking these settings to your liking.

The goal of this book is marketing with Facebook and is not meant to be an all encompassing reference to using Facebook. Therefore, I haven't covered every single feature in Facebook—it is the features described in this chapter that run throughout the entire platform. It is important to understand how this framework contributes to Facebook.

Figure 2.28   The Settings feature that allows you to control nearly every aspect of your Facebook account.

Establishing a Corporate Presence

A corporation can develop a strong presence on Facebook in multiple ways. If you are an executive within a corporation, you might question why any company would want a presence on a social network that seems so personal in nature. If you don't want to fish in a pond that is packed with approximately 800,000 new fish every single day, then have fun somewhere else. I, of course, say that with some sarcasm. I do understand that some companies resist using Facebook for business purposes.

Facebook: Personal or Professional?

Facebook has, for most of its history, been seen as a personal social network. On Facebook you can let your hair down a little and interact with your college buddies, family, and close friends. You share pictures and videos from recent vacations or of your baby's first steps. You post your personal opinions on random topics such as your favorite pizza toppings or who/what is annoying you today. If you want to do any business networking, there is LinkedIn. On LinkedIn you can input your resume, get recommendations, and set up a Group around your company, product, service, or industry and several other business-related activities. The problem here, as is the case with every other social network currently, is that Facebook is growing at such a fast pace that you can't ignore it. Facebook is currently growing at the rate of a completely new LinkedIn user base every 4 weeks or so.

What has been interesting when comparing personal versus professional networks has been the move by some companies to allow access to LinkedIn but deny access to Facebook, Twitter, MySpace, or other social networks.

Right now you're probably wondering why we're even talking about personal versus professional personas. Everyone has both personal and professional lives that they separate. You're a different person on the weekends around your family and friends than you are when sitting across the boardroom from your boss, customers, or vendors. Right?

Surely, I understand the hesitation between whether you should blend your personal and professional lives. Some people, myself included, have decided that everything we do is our life. We don't distinguish, for the most part, between a personal and professional life. I want business partners to know my personal interests in the Red Sox, Jay-Z, gadgets, and everything else that I am a fan of or have an interest in. People from both my personal and professional lives can see pictures from my wedding or my recent vacation. For me, it translates into a lot of business.

People can establish a 360-degree view of who I am. They can get to know me as an individual before we ever meet at a networking event or have a conference call about a potential partnership. We can interact on a personal level that might lead to establishing a professional relationship. After all, at our professional core, we prefer to do business with friends. We trust our friends and hope that our friends trust us. We would never want to do anything against our friends that might disappoint them, put them into a precarious position, or hurt them. Therefore, we tend to work harder when we do business with friends. It is usually more enjoyable and easier as well. Facebook provides the perfect opportunity for this to occur.

This blending of personal and professional also helps to develop a strong community, real friends, and interesting conversations. However, not everyone feels comfortable with, or has the ability, to make that melding between their personal and professional lives. But, even if you don't want to cross these two areas of your lifestyle with one another, and you prefer to keep Facebook personal and LinkedIn professional, you still should consider establishing a corporate presence.

Developing a Corporate Facebook Presence

Besides the individual choice of whether to join Facebook and blend your personal and professional lives, the reason why, as a brand, you want to consider establishing a presence on Facebook is because it helps to humanize your brand. Facebook is a very personal social network. It provides the perfect opportunity to help humanize your brand. Through the types of content that you can choose to share on a Facebook Page or Group, you can show that your company is a lot more than just a logo. You can peel back that logo to expose all the great personalities that make up your company.

Facebook is a thriving community in which there are sure to be fans of your company, executives, product, or service. If you're shaking your head left and right yelling loudly that you don't have any fans, realize that your prospects, customers, and future fans are hanging out on Facebook. Developing a presence on Facebook provides you the opportunity to bubble up these fans and activate them by providing them with a community in which they can interact with one another and with your company. You need to realize that the days of forcing your prospects, customers, and fans of your brand to go to a website of *your* choosing is gone. Sure, you can still drive traffic to your website and convert people through a contact or informational form. There is still a lot of value in corporate websites. But, nowadays, you have to go where your prospects, customers, and fans hang out and build communities with them there. This, in turn, can turn toward visiting your corporate website and engaging with you on your turf. If you ignore that, you are missing valuable opportunities to develop a stronger community. For instance, if I only hang out on Facebook and you only hang out on MySpace or Twitter, you're missing an opportunity to engage with me, even though I could be speaking your praises or running your name through the mud on Facebook.

With Facebook continuing to grow more and more in popularity, it makes sense to develop a corporate presence. At the very least, establishing even a basic presence on Facebook can make it more difficult for others to claim your brand on Facebook. If you need even more convincing, realize that Facebook is now the top driver of traffic, over Google, to large sites.

Getting Started

So now that I've convinced you to establish a corporate presence, how do you get started? What do you need to know? What about someone stealing your brand's name? Is that possible? What if someone says something bad about you on Facebook? Will that show up? What are *fans*? What's the ROI of our efforts? How much time do we need to spend to make it useful? All these are questions that come up when corporations consider venturing onto Facebook. Therefore, if any of those questions ran through your head, trust me, you're not alone. In fact, I bet that those questions are then followed by: "I don't want my employees on Facebook all day." "If they're on Facebook, how will I control them from going on their personal pages, chatting with their friends, or checking out pictures from their friends' party last weekend." "I can't afford to give my employees time to "hang out" on Facebook." "I need them working on their projects."

 Tip

One of the easiest ways for companies to begin developing a corporate presence is to ensure that your employees use the same name for the company in their profiles. When a company is first created by a user, it is saved into Facebook's database so that when other employees join they can find and use a standardized company name. This helps to link employees together and allow users to search for you based on a company search.

This tip is helpful to find other employees, especially if you have a large organization or one that might be decentralized with employees working from all over the world. This does not allow your employees to connect in a centralized area. Furthermore, it doesn't do anything to help your prospects and customers. To assist with this, Facebook has created two different areas: Pages and Groups.

Facebook Pages

Facebook describes Pages as "a voice to any public figure or organization to join the conversation with Facebook users...a public profile lets users connect to what they care about." Facebook Pages are used by celebrities, bands, sports teams, corporations, films, nonprofits, and those users who have exceeded the friends limit on their personal profile pages.

When Facebook originally launched Fan Pages, it had limited features and looked different than regular profiles. However, as more people flocked to Fan Pages, Facebook changed from Fan Pages to Pages and updated them so that they now resemble a regular profile. Pages allow the administrator to customize the tabs, add in basic information, and control whether fans can post on the wall, upload photos and videos, and other security controls.

One of the biggest changes to the Pages was when Facebook created the Facebook Markup Language (FBML). Besides the other features of FBML, one of the ways that it can be used is to alter the look, feel, and behavior of Pages. Some of the best examples of Pages are described in Chapter 10, "Best in Class," on the Best in Class users, Pages, and Groups.

Getting Started with Your Facebook Page

Now that you've decided to create a Facebook Page for your company, similar to the setting up of your personal profile, you should take a number of steps to ensure your Page is set up properly. The following are some tips to help you get started:

1. **Claim your Facebook Page**—The first step is to claim, classify, and get your Facebook Page created. One of the easiest ways to do this is to search for a Facebook Page that is already created. Scroll to the bottom, and in the left corner, you notice a link that says "Create a Page for My Business," as shown in Figure 3.1. Click on that link to start the process.

Figure 3.1   Create a Page for My Business in the bottom left corner of Facebook's Pages allows you to set up your own Facebook Page.

That link is going to take you to the Create New Facebook Page section of the website (see Figure 3.2). Choose the best classification for your Page, whether you want to be classified as a local business, brand, product, organization, artist, band, or public figure. Depending on your choice, you need to choose one more level of classification.

Next, provide the name of your organization. Ensure that this is the name that you want to appear as your Facebook Page. You can't change the name after it's completed. Your only option will be to delete it and start all over again. (Trust me, I know from experience.) When you have carefully selected and typed in your name, you need to confirm that you have authorization to create the Page by providing an electronic signature.

Figure 3.2 To create a Facebook Page you must choose a category classification that best suits your brand, product, service, or person.

You are now ready to start setting up your Page. One thing you'll find different compared to the personal profiles is that your Page will not be published publicly until you select the option to publish it. That means that you can spend time branding your Page, configuring all the options, and tweaking to your liking before letting the rest of the world see it. Put your best foot forward to start out and then continue to improve as time goes on.

2. **Configure settings**—Again, similar to the personal profiles, Facebook allows you to configure a lot of settings (see Figure 3.3). Take some time to run through each of the sections and tweak to your liking.

Figure 3.3 The multitude of settings available for Facebook Pages.

3. **Upload your logo**—Because this Page is set up as an extension of your brand on Facebook, you need to use your corporate logo as your default

profile picture. Adjust the size of your logo so that the thumbnail version that will be created and used by Facebook shows your entire logo. This thumbnail version will be shown besides all your status updates; therefore, you want your full logo, if possible, to be visible. See Figures 3.4 and 3.5 for the incorrect and the correct way to do it.

Figure 3.4   The Wine Library TV Facebook Page, which has done a great job by uploading its logo as its default profile image but hasn't adjusted it to fit the thumbnail view correctly.

Figure 3.5   The Advance Guard Facebook Page, which uploaded its logo as its default profile image but also configured its image so the full logo displays as the thumbnail.

4. **Add the Notes tab**—If your company has a blog, you can pull in the RSS feed through the Notes feature (see Figure 3.6). If your company doesn't have a blog, first, you should take steps to change that. Second, you can pull in any other RSS that your company might have, such as a Corporate News section on your website.

Figure 3.6 Similar to the Notes tab on the personal profiles, Facebook Pages also allows you to activate a Notes tab that you can pull in your external RSS feed.

 Tip

Because the Notes feature in Facebook is limited in settings and features that you can control, you might also want to consider pulling in your RSS feed through one of the many RSS applications that are available. These RSS applications allow a more in-depth experience and interaction level with the blog posts that are pulled in. These applications also give you more settings to control when and how your posts are sucked into the application and then displayed on Facebook (see Figure 3.7).

Figure 3.7 One of the many RSS feed applications that can be integrated with your Facebook Page. Most of these applications provide a richer feature set that the Notes feature doesn't allow.

5. **Upload photos**—Do you have photos of your offices, your staff, or anything else related to your company? Create a couple of photo

albums and upload the photos for everyone to see. Remember, not only are you trying to establish a presence on Facebook for your brand, but you're also trying to humanize your brand. One of the easiest ways to do this is by showing the people and physical office spaces that help your company to function on a daily basis (see Figure 3.8). Also, if your office space sucks, it might be good motivation to switch things up a little.

Figure 3.8   The Ridge at Blue Hills luxury apartment community outside of Boston, MA. The Ridge uses its Facebook Page to show people pictures of the property without forcing them to leave Facebook and go to its website.

Additionally, if you have photos of your products, especially in action, or screenshots of your software, create an album for them as well. You can provide a short description of each photo or screenshot; therefore, it's a good way to continue informing people that land on your Facebook Page before you try moving them off and over to your website or another landing page. You have to hang out where everyone else feels comfortable hanging out. That means that if your prospects, customers, and fans enjoy hanging out on Facebook, you should provide all the resources possible on your Facebook Page for them. One of the ways you can do this is by uploading photos and screenshots of your products or services.

6. **Upload videos**—Do you have client testimonials, product demos, behind-the-scenes videos of your operations, commercials, or interviews? Activate the Video tab and upload them all to your Facebook Page (see Figure 3.9). To be fair, it is important that you know that uploading videos is a much longer process than uploading photos. But, it is another great form of media that you can share with your

prospects, customers, fans, and even, employees. If you're not streamlining all these videos already on your corporate website, your Facebook Page is a good place to bring these videos that are splintered all across the Internet together in one place.

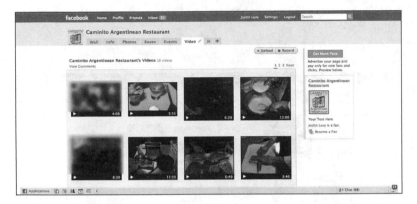

Figure 3.9 At my restaurant, Caminito Argentinean Steakhouse, we have created a Facebook Page where we upload instructional videos directly into Facebook. We also post these videos as "Prime Cuts TV" on other video services.

 Tip

Have you already uploaded these videos to YouTube? If so, you can install many different YouTube applications on your Page (see Figure 3.10). These applications pull in links to your YouTube videos. Many of them allow you to view the videos on your Facebook Page. None of them though actually transfer the video file to the Videos section of your Facebook Page. There is nothing wrong with that, but I want to save you from hunting for hours for an application that does that.

There are actually many benefits from taking the route of uploading your videos to YouTube and then porting them into your Facebook Page. First, you can use a service such as TubeMogul and actually push your videos out to many different video services, including YouTube, to extend the reach of them. You can then port these videos from YouTube onto your Facebook Page. That way, you serve your video up on many different video platforms and extend the reach of them and the number of online communities that you share the video on.

7. **Set up the Events tab**—If your company hosts events, puts on webinars, throws meetups or any other online and offline event, you should

Figure 3.10   Some of the many YouTube applications available to integrate with your Facebook Page. Most of these applications allow you to pull in the videos that you're already posting to YouTube and play them directly from your Facebook Page.

create an event within Facebook to ensure your Facebook Page is classi-fied as the organizer (see Figure 3.11). This allows users on Facebook to register for the event and share it into their news streams to help extend the reach of the event. If you use an online event registration service such as Eventbrite (eventbrite.com), it actually allows you to create a Facebook Event directly from Eventbrite so that you don't need to spend time duplicating the information.

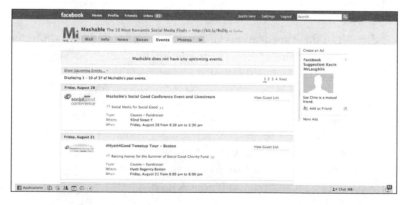

Figure 3.11   Mashable, a social media blog and one of the top rated blogs in the world, utilized the Events tab of its Facebook Page to show where it's holding meetups, parties, and other events around the country.

8. **Explore applications**—There are a bunch of applications that you can use to help customize your Facebook Page (see Figure 3.12). If you're a restaurant, there are applications such as OpenTable and Zagat Ratings that you could integrate. If you or someone else from your company does a lot of public speaking, you can upload your slide decks to

Slideshare.net and then integrate their Facebook application onto your Page. If your company is active on Twitter, you can find applications that allow you to create a tab on your Page dedicated to your Twitter stream. There are also applications for photo services such as Flickr, video services such as YouTube, polls such as Poll Daddy, as we've previously discussed, calendar publishing apps, and thousands other options that can help you to customize your Page.

Figure 3.12   The Applications page where you can browse a library of applications to integrate with your Facebook Page.

Although all these applications enable you to customize the options and information on your Facebook Page, one application allows you to totally change the look and feel of your Facebook Page: the Facebook Static FBML application. FBML is best described by Wikipedia as

> "...a variant-evolved subset of HTML with some elements removed.... It is the specification of how to encode content so that Facebook's servers can read and publish it, which is needed in the Facebook-specific feed so that Facebook's system can properly parse content and publish it as specified."

What that essentially means is that FBML is a simplified HTML coding language that enables you to mock up custom widgets or tabs on your Facebook Page (see Figure 3.13).

This is beneficial to companies, celebrities, and public figures because it allows you to brand your Page with your specific colors, provide a similar layout to your other websites, and provide rich content on your

Figure 3.13 The FBML edit screen where you can add custom, simplified HTML that allows you to tweak and customize your Facebook Page.

Facebook Page. Several of the Best in Class Pages discussed in Chapter 10 have utilized FBML. Check out how some of those Pages have utilized this application and then consider getting someone to do a little coding for you.

9. **Activate the Discussions tab**—To help foster community and drive conversations, Facebook has a Discussions feature that you can activate and add to your Page (see Figure 3.14). This is essentially a customized forums board hosted on your Facebook Page, which is a great way to start and continue conversations, provide information, and interact with your prospects, customers, and fans. Of course, you can interact with them directly on the Wall, but the Discussions feature allows you (or others) to seed questions that the rest of the community can easily join in on. If you're not already running a forums board elsewhere on the Internet, this is a good way to dip your toe in. Even if you run forums board on another service, this is a great way to get some conversations going.

Figure 3.14 The Discussions tab on The Ellen DeGeneres Show Facebook Page.

10. **Publish your Page**—Last, but not least, you need to publish your Facebook Page after you tweak the settings and applications, and added in, possibly, some customization using the capabilities of FBML. Don't worry if it's not perfect. It's not meant to be perfect. If you waited to publish your Facebook Page, your corporate website, your blog, your product, or anything else until it is "perfect," you would never get around to actually publishing anything. You would be stuck in the cycle of forever tweaks, always finding something wrong that needs to be adjusted.

What's Next

So, you've now decided to start a Facebook Page for your business; you've spent some time customizing it; and you've now published it. "Now what?" you might ask yourself. If you asked yourself that question, fantastic. If not, you should. Not even the biggest brands and most popular celebrities in the world just have their fans suddenly start finding them on Facebook because they've published their Page, unless of course, you're Justin Timberlake, Beyonce, or the new teen group of the year. That begs the question: "How do I get people to my Page?"

One of the first things you should do is to create an easy-to-remember URL that redirects to your Facebook Page. Facebook allows you to create a custom URL, sometimes called a "vanity URL" so that the URL is http://facebook.com/YourBrand. But, you must have 100 fans before that option kicks into play. While you're waiting to get to 100+ fans, you can either create a URL that is a subdomain of your website, such as http://facebook.mysite.com, or you can use a URL shortening service and create a customized shortened URL such as: http://bit.ly/brandfb. Whichever option you choose, make sure it's easy-to-remember because you'll never remember the direct default URL to your Facebook Page if it is something like what is shown in Figure 3.15.

The next thing you should do is promote your Facebook Page. You can start in a number of ways.

Promoting Your Facebook Page
Email Signature

Adjust your email signature to include your Facebook Page, as shown in Figure 3.16. This is among the simplest tweaks you can make and will reach a lot of people, especially if you're someone that sends a lot of emails.

Figure 3.15 Before you can obtain a custom URL for your Facebook Page, the URL will be a long combination of your Page name, numbers, and some other characters.

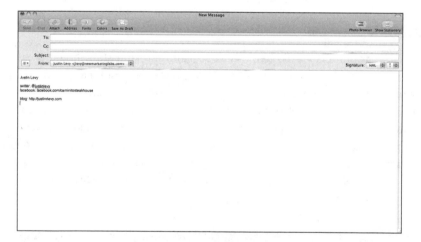

Figure 3.16 Promoting your Facebook Page in your email signature. There are many services available that add a Facebook logo and hyperlink as well.

Twitter

Begin promoting your Facebook Page on Twitter, as shown in Figure 3.17. Don't spam your Twitter followers but occasionally letting them know, maybe a few times per week, that they can also connect with you on your Facebook Page can help to drive more attention to it. Also, if they enjoy connecting more on Facebook than on Twitter, you will more likely have better, more in-depth conversations with them over on your Page. You should also encourage any other employees or members of your team who also have Twitter accounts to begin promoting that you now have a Facebook Page. This is where having an easy-to-remember URL can is very handy.

Figure 3.17   An example of promoting your Facebook Page on Twitter.

Facebook

Similar to promoting via Twitter, you, your team, and your staff should use the Share feature on Facebook to occasionally share the Facebook Page into their news stream. You can also send an email within Facebook encouraging your friends to become fans of your Facebook Page, as shown in Figure 3.18. This is easy to do but be careful not to do it too often. It is a source of annoyance to many users on Facebook because people "pimp" their Facebook Page a little too often. If you don't interact on your personal Wall often, you shouldn't share your Facebook Page onto your wall too often. The last thing you want is for your Wall to be consumed only with you "pimping" your Facebook Page.

Figure 3.18   Facebook allows you the ability to suggest your Facebook Page to your personal friends.

Similarly, with sending emails through Facebook requesting people to become a fan of your Page, you can send the request a couple times, but if people don't become fans after that, you should get the message and realize that any more requests that you send them will seem like spam to them and will only annoy them with you and your brand. You definitely don't want that to happen.

Email Marketing

If your company sends out email marketing such as newsletters, company updates, or anything like that, you should have a call-to-action in every email campaign that encourages people to interact with you on your Facebook Page. When you first launch your Page, you might include an article in your newsletter about it and encourage people to fan you. After that, you should have that information in a static sidebar or in the signature section of your email creatives (see Figure 3.19).

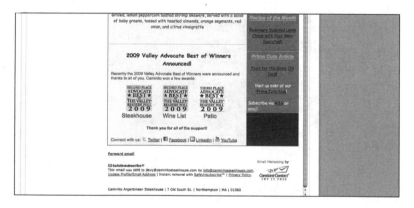

Figure 3.19   An example of incorporating a Connect with Us section of your email newsletter in which you encourage your subscribers to connect with you via your Facebook Page (and other social networks).

Company Website

Similar to your email marketing, you should show off the various social networks that you're active in, including your Facebook Page. You can do this by creating a separate tab and/or a sidebar widget on all the pages of your website where visitors can link out to (see Figure 3.20).

Alternatively, if you want to call out your Facebook Page a little more, you can add a Fan Box to your website. The Fan Box can allow people to fan your Facebook Page directly from your website or blog, see the other people that are fans of your Facebook Page, and interact with the Page (see Figure 3.21).

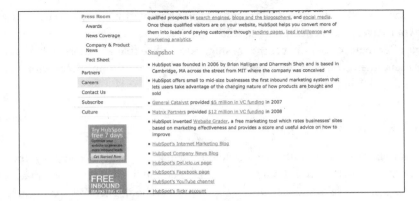

Figure 3.20 Another easy way to encourage people to connect with you via your Facebook Page is to add a link to your website. HubSpot, an inbound marketing company based in Cambridge, MA, chooses to promote its social networks on its Press Room.

Figure 3.21 Coca-Cola visibly promotes its Facebook Page by integrating the Fan Box into its website.

Facebook Ads

You can run targeted Facebook ads that appear in the right sidebar area of users' Facebook accounts with a message to encourage them to fan your Page. We discuss Facebooks Ads in greater detail in Chapter 5, "Facebook Advertising: How and Why You Should Be Using It." But, suffice it to say that running a Facebook Ad as promotion of your Page is a cheap method to get your Page in front of a targeted group of Facebook users, as shown in Figure 3.22.

Google AdWords

Similar to running a Facebook Ad, if you want to spend some money on attracting fans, you can run Google AdWords with the call-to-action being to fan your

Figure 3.22   Promote your Facebook Page by creating a targeted ad using the Facebook Ads system.

Facebook Page. You might offer some type of special reward, contest, or something else to grab the person's attention. Although I haven't personally seen this used often, if ever, it is a possibility. But, if I were going to spend money with Google AdWords, it would more than likely be to push people to my website that would have a call-to-action to become a fan of my Page through the Fan Box. That way, I keep the traffic and get the eyes on my website, not Facebook. With hundreds of millions of users, they get enough traffic...no need helping them get more.

As with many of the tips and strategies throughout this book, you can promote your Facebook Page in other ways. You can also promote via commercials, radio spots, newspaper or magazine ads, or a number of other traditional forms of advertising. It all depends on what your company is already doing for advertising, marketing, and engagement with your prospects and customers. At the end of the day, simply try to integrate the promotion of your Facebook Page wherever it makes sense within your advertising and marketing plans, in much the same manner you would as your website or other contact information.

Facebook Groups

Whereas Pages are the public watering holes for fans of your brand, Facebook Groups are where you can set up private communities for your company, both internally or externally.

Facebook Pages are designed to provide companies, celebrities, or other public figures with the ability to establish a presence to allow them to interact publicly with their fans, prospects, or customers (see Figure 3.23). However, some times you want a private area in which you can engage a select group of customers or a special area just for your employees. This is where Facebook Groups come into play.

Figure 3.23   Behind-the-scenes of a Facebook Group: This example shows #journchat, a weekly conversation that takes place on Twitter among journalists, bloggers, and public relations professionals.

A Facebook Group can be best described as "a real-life interest or group or to declare an affiliation or association with people and things...you are creating a community of people and friends to promote, share and discuss relevant topics."

You can set up a Facebook Group with one of three different levels of access:

- **Open**—Anyone can join.

- **Closed**—You must request to join the Group, and it must be approved by the administrator.

- **Secret**—You must be invited into the Group, and the Group doesn't show up in any searches.

These different levels of access can be beneficial when deciding *why* you want to set up your Group. If you're a smaller company and want to have a private area for your employees to engage, you might make the Group secret. However, if you're a large company and want to have an area for employees to hang out, you might set the level of access to closed so that you can decide who gets in.

Facebook Groups are usually used around a particular issue. But, as you can see, a Group can be used in a few uniques ways and for corporate use, too.

In October 2009, Facebook transformed the format and functionality of Groups to be more similar to Pages. They now look and feel the exact same way including posting updates to your News Feed, thus leaving little differences between the two. The one major difference is that you can't install applications or extend functionality with FBML coding in Groups like you can with Pages. This limits the usefulness of Groups compared to Pages. There are conversations taking place online suggesting that Facebook should merge Pages and Groups together. So far, all signs point to this merger; however, one never knows what Facebook will do until they implement it.

Many of the concepts that have been discussed previously regarding Facebook Pages are pertinent to Facebook Groups as well, so make sure you revisit the instructions and tips above to properly set up your Group.

Page or Group: Which One?

It is understandable that you might be a bit confused after reading this chapter and trying to figure out how to properly brand your company on Facebook and start engaging with your prospects, customers, employees, and fans. Both the Pages and Groups features within Facebook have many benefits. Which one should you choose and why?

Generally, if you're a brand, organization, celebrity, politician, or other public figure, and you want to engage with your prospects, customers, and fans, you want to set up a Facebook Page. Pages are public. That means that all features of the Page can be seen without having to become a fan of it. Everyone can join your Page and can promote it into their news feed. Furthermore, the available features and level of customization is unparalleled when comparing it with the capabilities of Groups. This isn't because Facebook has decided to neglect Groups. Facebook Pages are designed for brands, celebrities, and other public figures to be encouraged to set up public presences on the network. This is why in March 2009, Facebook made the decision to convert Pages into having a similar look, feel, and functionality of personal profiles. Facebook wants this to be another place for your brand besides your company website. For those that choose to embrace this, it can prove to be beneficial. In fact, a paidContent.org post in May 2009 states that Facebook has overtaken Google as the top referrer to large websites.

For all intents and purposes, a brand is equivalent to a person in Facebook. Also, because Pages are public, they're also visible to search engines.

Groups are private and you must request access to join the group. This feature is good if you want to have private discussions with a select group of people. A group is good for brands that might want to set up a private community but lack funds to have an enterprise-level community developed. A group is also good for companies that want a quick, private community for their team or a select group of customers. Although I'd be careful of sharing sensitive data on Facebook because you don't control what happens with that information, it is an easy way to set up a private community quickly. You might start a Group that you invite select customers into for feedback purposes and discussion around an upcoming product or release, or allow direct access to particular individuals within your organization. If you choose to set one up for your employees, it is an easy way to communicate with your them.

Nurturing Your Community

Now that you have decided which type of community you want to build, either a Facebook Page, Group, or both, and you spent some time tweaking the settings and building up your community, you need to continue to nurture it. What should you do? Just post some status updates from time to time? That seems kind of lame, huh? This seems to be one of the top questions received by companies after they set up a Facebook Page or Group. It's understandable. On the surface, when you set everything up, besides keeping things tidy and updated, it can seem difficult to see how you might nurture and continue to strengthen your community. Take a few of the following thoughts into consideration.

Run Contests or Sweepstakes

A sure-fire way to get engagement by your community is to run contests or sweepstakes that are available only to your Facebook community, as shown in Figure 3.24. The simplest and fastest way to do this is by encouraging responses to a particular question or discussion topic. You can offer a free month of service, a discount on your online store, and more.

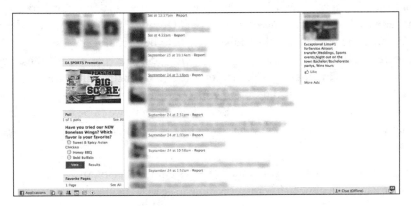

Figure 3.24 Encourage engagement and "stickiness" to your Facebook Page by running contests or sweepstakes on your Page.

Share Specific Content

You should share some amount of content that is shared only with your Facebook community (see Figure 3.25). This is especially important if you interact with some of these same people in other online communities such as Twitter, MySpace, LinkedIn, or a private social network. By sharing unique content with your Facebook community, they will be encouraged to return often. They will also be encouraged to begin engaging within the community because it's content that they can't find elsewhere in other areas in which the two of you might connect.

Figure 3.25   Share specific content on your Facebook Page that isn't just ported from another service such as Twitter. The McDonald's team does a great job of sharing content on its Facebook Page.

Create Specific Content

Facebook offers many ways that you can create content that is specific only to your Facebook communities (see Figure 3.26). Instead of always just porting in your YouTube videos, or uploading videos that you have also uploaded to other video services, how about creating some videos directly within Facebook? Upload some new product designs and share them on Facebook exclusively first. Maybe leave them up there for a week or so before you then also upload them to other photo services. If your fans, prospects, and customers know they might receive exclusive content by staying engaged with your Facebook community, they will be more likely to return.

Figure 3.26   Create content that is specific only to your Facebook Page. This is an example of Chris Brogan, author of *Trust Agents*, sharing a video with the fans of the Trust Agents Facebook Page.

Simply Engage

One of the easiest steps you can take is to simply engage your Facebook community (see Figure 3.27). Don't just spend all this time creating this fantastic community and then leave it to rely on only receiving automatic updates from pumped in RSS feeds, YouTube, or Flickr applications. Come hang out in your community. Update your status once or twice a day. Use a status update to ask your community how their day is going or their thoughts on a question. Make a few comments back to some of the people who have taken the time out of their busy day to engage there with you. Again, this sounds simple but is so often overlooked and neglected. Just being there puts you far ahead of a lot of other companies, possibly even your competition.

Figure 3.27   Engage often by asking questions and becoming involved with your community. The Food Network engages a lot via their Facebook Page generating hundreds of comments whenever it asks a question.

These are just a few of the many ideas that you can use to help keep your community engaged. Communities, generally, don't manage themselves. They need someone around to keep prodding them through engagement, stimulating conversations, and various forms of content. The more often you can do that with your community, the more of a nurtured, vibrant, active community you will have on Facebook. This becomes even more important if you decide to set up a Facebook Page instead of a Group because all this engagement will be public to everyone, not just the members of your community.

As we start talking about all this engagement, I can sense some hesitation starting to build up. I know exactly what you're worried about. You're worried that someone will post something negative on your Wall about you. You're worried that you will be mocked, ridiculed, or hated on for one reason or another. You want to know how you can control for that.

Should You Police Your Community?

The issue of negative comments is one that every brand who signs up for a Facebook Page has to deal with. Although this could be an issue within a Group, especially if it is around an industry topic that might cause some level of debate, you will more likely feel this concern around Facebook Pages. The reason being, of course, that the comments or content is public. It can be seen by all.

Of course, with the hundreds of millions of users, some people have probably had a bad experience with your company. Although in an ideal world only positive information would be talked about publicly by others, this certainly is not the case. Many corporations when I meet with them for the first time are weary of knowing what people are saying about them. What you don't know can't hurt you. Right? Wrong. These conversations are taking place 24 hours per day, and your ability to find them and respond is critical.

So, someone posts something negative on your Wall, what do you do? Easy, right? Just delete it and move on. You want only the positive and fun content around your community. Makes perfect sense. Except if you do this, you'll be committing a cardinal sin of online brand engagement.

There are going to be people, both online and offline, who are not happy with your brand, product, or service for one reason or another. Online they can leave comments within your various online outposts, such as your Facebook Page or Group. If the comment isn't violent, overly disruptive, or continual, leave the comment alone. You then have to make the decision whether to respond to the comment. Both decisions have positives and negatives. On one hand, if you do respond, it could spark a never-ending back and forth that might only add lighter fluid to a smoldering fire that would have otherwise put itself out. However, on the other side of the coin, if you don't respond, you appear as though you're ignoring the person or complaint she is bringing to your attention. This could also have an adverse effect. The best advice is to judge each comment on a case-by-case basis. Some you'll respond to whereas others you're going to make the decision that it's best to leave it alone.

To monitor and respond to any comments about your executives, company, industry, or competitors, plenty of professional grade tools, such as Radian6 (www. radian6.com), are available. Radian6 enables you to actively measure mainstream news, blogs, blog comments, forums, forum replies, and, currently, micromedia sites that include Twitter and FriendFeed. One of the downfalls of Facebook being a closed platform is that tools such as Radian6 can't "see" behind the walls to monitor the conversations that are taking place. However, it will be interesting to see how Facebook continues to extend its new search feature and how it decides to integrate FriendFeed. FriendFeed is currently one of the sites that tools such as Radian6 can measure. The other issue is that you can't grab an RSS feed or set up an email alert to trigger based on criteria that you plug into Facebook. This is bound to happen now that Facebook is going through the process of integrating FriendFeed in and making lots of other platform enhancements, I think we'll see the search capabilities extend to RSS or email alerts.

While we wait for some type of RSS or alert capabilities arrive to the Facebook platform, you should run searches from time to time. Run searches for your company, executives, products, services, and industry. This can give you an idea of what, if anything, is said within the Walls of Facebook. Though not perfect, it is a start to monitoring the conversations taking place around you on Facebook. For everything else, I'd strongly consider setting up a listening and monitoring tool such as Radian6. If you just want to dip your feet in, you could start by setting up Google Alerts and custom Twitter Searches around the terms that matter to you.

Extending Facebook into the Interwebs: The Power and Reach of Facebook Connect

As we continue to explore Facebook, the majority of the focus, as you would expect, is on the ways in which you can use Facebook from within Facebook. That's exactly what Facebook wants from you. The more useful features that exist within Facebook, the more you'll come back, the longer you'll stay, and the more people you'll tell about how great it is. Facebook has spent a lot of time building a feature set geared toward addicting you to its service. It is a wonderful loop of engagement that Facebook creates. But, at the same time, Facebook also has a want and need to continue growing its user base.

Although 400+ million people is a lot, it still isn't *everyone*. Therefore, Facebook must continually come up with new ways to find users. Also, as it's out searching for new users, it also wants to ensure that it entices back its current user base as often as possible.

This provides more opportunities for you, as a marketer, because it increases the possibility for you to connect with new prospects, current customers, and fans of your brand.

To accomplish all these goals, Facebook created Facebook Connect, which was released in December 2008. If you've visited practically any major website or even most top blogs, you've inevitably seen an implementation of Facebook Connect, even if you didn't realize it. Facebook Connect has been implemented on over 80,000 websites with more than 60 million users on a monthly basis. That means its more widespread than you ever notice.

Facebook Connect is a lot more than just a blue "Connect with Facebook" box that lets you sign in with your Facebook credentials instead of registering for the site. Facebook gives a basic and geeky definition of Facebook Connect, calling it: "a powerful set of APIs for developers that lets users bring their identity and connections everywhere." Facebook Connect is a powerful tool with a complex set of features that can be integrated into websites. For marketers, integrating Facebook Connect helps to bring more eyes to your website thus giving you more opportunities to connect and convert as well as giving you the ability to implement other features available within Facebook Connect. Additionally, it provides more resources to the user who visits your website and doesn't need to create a new log in just to leave a comment or interact with your website in some other way.

However, these implementations don't even begin to touch on the capabilities of Facebook Connect. Let's take a little time to walk through some of the features of Facebook Connect along with a couple examples. From that you should have a few ideas on how you may want to integrate Facebook Connect with your website or blog.

Using Facebook Connect for Commenting

The integration of Facebook Connect for commenting is probably the single most-popular feature used on websites. This feature allows users to choose to sign in with their Facebook account credentials to post comments on a blog or website. Several blog and commenting platforms (such as Disqus, shown in Figure 4.1) have integrated Facebook Connect into their platforms, meaning that users of the blog and commenting system can easily add Facebook Connect to their sites. This has helped to increase engagement with Facebook Connect for commenting. According to one of the most popular blogs in the world, The Huffington Post, it has seen more than one-third of new commenters come through Facebook.

Figure 4.1   Commenting system Disqus provides tight integration of Facebook Connect, featuring the ability to allow users to leave comments.

Using Facebook Connect to Provide Sharing Options

Another common feature that you probably don't realize comes from an implementation of Facebook Connect is the ability to share an article from a blog or website on Facebook (see Figure 4.2). There are plugins and tools such as "Share This" and "Add This" that have Facebook as a sharing option among several other social networks such as Twitter; however, when Facebook is added to a website as a standalone option, it takes Facebook Connect to make everything work smoothly. With the click of a button, a pop-up or new tab opens and automatically adds the link from the story. You then have the option of adding in some additional text as you normally would with a status update; then you can publish that link to your Wall.

Sharing Stories into Your Stream with Facebook Connect

The ability to share stories into your stream is a feature of some more socially forward websites such as Yelp (see Figure 4.3). On Yelp, once you rate a restaurant, you're able to push that review and restaurant information to your Wall as a status update. Where this differs from the Share functionality is that with the Share feature, you're sharing an article from a website or blog. With the ability to stream stories, you're able to automatically push information to your Facebook Wall while you're interacting on other websites. This is beneficial to the websites that are able to integrate it because the stream story usually carries some of the branding from the website such as a logo thus bringing increased brand awareness.

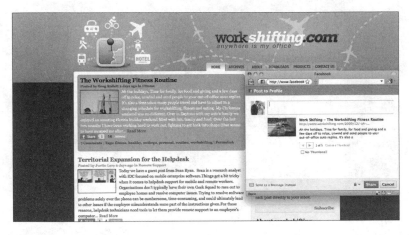

Figure 4.2   By implementing Facebook Share using Facebook Connect, you can allow users to easily share stories they find interesting with their Facebook community, thus increasing the reach of your article or blog post.

Figure 4.3   Yelp allows users to share reviews of the services listed on their website with Facebook. This not only increases the reach and awareness of Yelp, it also increases the awareness of the service/business being reviewed.

Several websites allow you the option of publishing your activity to Facebook. You'll typically see this option with social networks and games that rely on users spreading information to bring awareness of their services. If you use popular social bookmarking website Delicious, you're able to use Facebook Connect to authorize Delicious to post the websites that you save to their service on your Facebook Wall. You can also add a Delicious box to your home page that will automatically update as you run around the web bookmarking websites.

By linking together the various places you enjoy hanging out around the Internet, you're able to use Facebook as a lifestream to show your community on Facebook what you're interested in. But, with that comes some cautionary advice: Ensure that the information that you're allowing to flow into Facebook doesn't overwhelm your community and is actually useful to *them*. If not then they'll begin hiding your status updates, ignoring you, de-fanning your Page, or at worse, unfriending you. If any of that happens then you close the door on everything that you've been working through this book to accomplish.

To help avoid flooding your community and understand how and where your activity on the Internet is used, it is helpful to create, what Louis Gray termed, a social media data flow.

Essentially, by working through this process you create a visual map of where the data that you input into various social networks ends up. This can help you get a grip on whether you may be overwhelming your community because it can happen easily as the habit of using Facebook Connect all over the web can become customary.

Recent Friend Activity

This feature of Facebook Connect allows you to see what your friends are doing within a website or application. You can see what your friends, family, or colleagues have commented on, uploaded, and shared or other ways that they've interacted with the website. An example of this is the integration that Joost (shown in Figure 4.4) has made.

Figure 4.4   Joost allows you to use Facebook Connect to see what your friends are watching on their services. This helps to create instant community and to keep users on the website longer because users will trust their friends' suggestions more.

Using Facebook Connect for Social Filtering

Similar to recent friend activity, the concept of social filtering is an interesting feature of Facebook Connect (see Figure 4.5). Essentially, the social filtering function allows you to see what your friends, who have connected to the website with their Facebook accounts, find popular, such as a concert.

Figure 4.5   By using social filtering, users on Digg can see the stories that are most relevant to their Facebook community.

Using Facebook Connect as a Single Sign On

The concept of single sign on is something that has continued to float around the Internet as users become increasingly frustrated with how many different websites they have to be signed up for to access content. Such concepts as OpenID have attempted to create a single sign on that people would use on all the websites they visit. The problem with OpenID though is that it requires website administrators to add OpenID functionality to their website. During the middle of this debate over single sign on, Facebook implemented Facebook Connect and instantly enabled 400+ million users to have a single sign on (see Figure 4.6). Yes, just like with OpenID, website administrators need to add additional code to their websites; however, unlike OpenID Facebook Connect also gives you access to the many other features that have been covered. Facebook Connect also moves ahead of OpenID and other single sign-on concepts because of Facebook's brand recognition.

By becoming a single sign-on resource, Facebook also benefits because users become more reliant on the social network. Because you have the ability to use Facebook to sign in to all your favorite websites, you're more likely to interact with

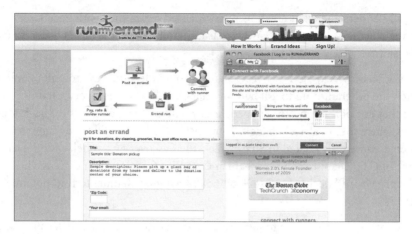

Figure 4.6   Facebook Connect enables users to use their Facebook profiles as a single form of identification to sign up/sign on to websites, such as runmyerrand.com.

Facebook more often. Even though you cannot access features of your Facebook account, and it wouldn't necessarily make sense for you to have the ability to, it does increase the amount that you interact with Facebook, increasing the likelihood that you'll actually head over to the social network and hang out over there as well.

Another beneficial feature of using Facebook Connect as a single sign on is that when you log in to Facebook either directly or connect with any site that uses Facebook Connect, Facebook signs you in to all the websites that you use Connect with. This means that if you visit five sites that use Facebook Connect, you will not be required to re-enter your login credentials multiple times. Also, that means that when you sign out of any one site, Facebook will sign you out of all websites. This can be helpful if you use a public computer so that you don't have to remember to log in and out of all the websites that you may visit during a browsing session.

As Facebook continues to grow, the concept of single sign on using Facebook Connect will become one of the, if not the, most popular feature of Facebook Connect.

Creating a Personalized Experience with Facebook Connect

The capability of Facebook Connect to create a personalized experience is something that we've only seen the tip of so far. Facebook Connect has the capability to use some of your information such as age, gender, location, or content that you've uploaded to Facebook to help create a story that has been created just for you.

To fully understand what creating a personalized experience with Facebook Connect actually means, it is easiest to learn about how some have chosen to use this feature.

During Shark Week, the Discovery Channel sought to find ways to pull people in to watch the programming that it had for Shark Week. The Discovery Channel realized that one of the ways to pull people in would be to reach out into the communities where they're already hanging out. Instead of hoping that they tune in and watch commercials related to Shark Week, the Discovery Channel, with the assistance of C.C. Chapman and his team at Campfire (previously known as The Advance Guard), decided to use Facebook as a digital channel to find potential viewers.

The easy way out would be to just use a Facebook Ad that had a slick call-to-action. No, that would be too simple. What if you could make users feel as though they were in a boat being attacked by a shark? What if you could make their heart race and make it really real for them? That would be cool, right? That is *exactly* what an application called Frenzied Waters created using Facebook Connect for Shark Week did. By using information that you've already made available to Facebook such as biographical information and photos, the Frenzied Waters application created an experience that made you feel as though you were part of the shark attack.

Another slick use of Facebook Connect was for the launch of the 10th anniversary of *Fight Club*, a movie featuring Brad Pitt. When you visit WelcomeToFC.com, you're prompted to enter your Facebook credentials. After you enter your credentials, the website (actually Facebook Connect) grabs data from your Facebook account such as your name, favorite movies, job information, and photos and uses it to build a story from *Fight Club* around you. At the end of the experience, it then encourages you to purchase the *Fight Club* DVD.

What both of these applications accomplish is invoking emotion and bringing you into the experience. This tends to hook you and makes you want to run around and share it with your friends because of how cool it is. This word-of-mouth marketing is the best type of marketing that any brand or product could ask for.

Integrating Chat Using the Live Feed

The Live Feed option enables users to chat live side-by-side with either streaming or static content on your website. Users access their Facebook accounts and use the status update feature to carry on conversations.

The Live Feed was first implemented and made uber famous during the Presidential Inauguration of Barack Obama (see Figure 4.7). During the Inauguration, CNN streamed the events live on CNN.com and, using Facebook Connect, allowed you to chat with your friends who were also watching on CNN.com.

Figure 4.7   CNN used the Live Feed to connect Facebook users with CNN content during the Presidential Inauguration of Barack Obama. The result: 4,000 status updates per minute and 136 million page views.

No one could have ever expected how many people would decide to take to CNN.com and start chatting away, sharing this once-in-a-lifetime experience, with their friends. According to Mashable.com

- CNN generated more than 136 million page views.

- More than 600,000 status updates posted through CNN.com to Facebook.

- During the broadcast more than 4,000 status updates occurred per minute being sent to Facebook from CNN.com.

- During the first minute of President Obama's inaugural speech, 8,500 status updates from CNN.com occurred.

This mind-blowing success led other event planners to turn to Facebook to enable conversations around their event. So far, the Live Feed has been used for the NBA All-Star game, the Michael Jackson Memorial, and a live viewing party of the finale of Bravo's "Real Housewives of New York City" among others.

In the future we will see many more large events integrate the Facebook Live Feed into their websites. Imagine watching the Olympics, attending a concert, watching the World Series, or watching a movie and chatting LIVE with all your friends who are also enjoying that same experience.

Whether you realize it, the Live Feed is similar to the Personalized Experience feature because it draws out emotion and connects us to something we can relate to. For the Personalized Experience, the tool creates an experience using information about ourselves to pull us into the application. The Live Feed connects us with our friends during a major event. By enabling this feature, the network hopes that we'll stay on their website longer, and Facebook ensures that we'll interact with their platform more. It also has the spin-off effect, much like Twitter hashtags around events, in that the rest of your network can see your status updates, wonder what you're up to, and hopefully join in on the fun.

Not Just for the Web

Although much of the discussion has been surrounding websites, where some of the features of Facebook Connect have really shone has been on the iPhone. Facebook Connect has become increasingly popular, especially among applications that offer reviews of entertainment and dining options such as movies, music, restaurants, bars, and hotels. Applications such as Flixster, a popular movie sharing and reviews application, have implemented Facebook Connect so that you can see how your friends on Facebook review a movie. Another popular iPhone application, UrbanSpoon, stated on the Facebook Connect Page: "When users sign in with Facebook Connect, they can find trusted referrals from friends on local favorites. 43,000 new users have connected to the app using Facebook. Those users have voted 150,000 times on restaurants, left 22,000 reviews, and uploaded 13,000 photos." The importance of this is not in the stats that UrbanSpoon reports, though it is impressive. Hone in on where UrbanSpoon refers to *trusted referrals*. This is the secret sauce for applications such as Flixster and UrbanSpoon (as shown in Figure 4.8) when they implement Facebook Connect.

Figure 4.8 UrbanSpoon uses Facebook Connect on both their website and their iPhone application. This allows users to read reviews from their friends instead of from users that are unknown to them.

In a society in which we're inundated with an estimated 35GB of data on a daily basis, we need to find ways to weed through all that information. One way doing exactly what we would do in our offline lives is to turn to friends, family, and colleagues for information. Instead of reading what the *New York Times* food critic thinks of the Italian spot across town, you now can turn to UrbanSpoon to see what *your* friends, family, or colleagues thought of it. Was the chicken parmigiana fantastic? Parking easy to find? Service horrible? Your friends on Facebook will tell you instantly. Where the payoff for the application comes in is that because it provides useful and trustworthy information, you'll keep coming back. If you know that you can turn to Flixster to watch movie trailers, find the closest movie theater to you, and show times and what your friends thought of the summer's supposed blockbuster, why wouldn't you keep coming back to Flixster?

A Few Stats

Facebook Connect was released in December 2008. After approximately only one year, Facebook Connect had been integrated, in one form or another, on more than 80,000 websites. On those 80,000 websites, approximately 60 million users have engaged with Facebook Connect. That means that, as of this writing, approximately 20 percent of all Facebook users utilize Facebook Connect on websites that they visit other than Facebook. It's no surprise that many of the largest websites have turned to integrating Facebook Connect to help drive more visitors and then translate those visitors into repeat traffic and increased engagement. According to Facebook, two-thirds of the top 100 websites in the United States and 50 percent of the world's top 100 websites have implemented Facebook Connect.

Summary

As you can see from the examples in this chapter, Facebook Connect can be a powerful tool to integrate into your website, blog, or application. Time and time again it has proven to drive increased traffic and engagement. What's nice about Facebook Connect is that you can select a wide breadth of options to integrate. You could begin immediately by implementing sharing of content on your website while you work on ways to integrate social filtering into your application and create a personalized experience for your visitors.

Beyond the capabilities that Facebook Connect allows you to implement, one of the most interesting aspects of Facebook Connect is that it provides you a social graph of your website, application, or service. Because of the information that Facebook knows about every user, you can identify exactly who is interacting with your website. Armed with that information you can create content, offers, and options geared to that demographic.

It is likely that Facebook will continue to expand Facebook Connect to include more options and flexibility.

5

Facebook Advertising: How and Why You Should Be Using It

You see them every time you log into Facebook. You head over to your profile or check your Facebook Page or Group, and you're greeted in the right sidebar with advertisements. Ever wondered how they get there? Ever wanted to figure out how they always know some personal bits of information about you such as your age or name? Want to learn how you can have an advertisement in the right sidebar? Welcome to Facebook advertising (see Figure 5.1).

Although Facebook provides many tools that you might find hard to understand how to use as part of your marketing campaign, one of the easiest tools to integrate into your marketing campaign is Facebook Ads.

Facebook has developed an advertising platform that is similar in many ways to Google AdWords. So, if you're familiar with how the Google AdWords platform works, then using Facebook Ads won't take long to get you up to speed on. However, where Facebook Ads differ from Google AdWords is that you can target your campaigns based on all the information that we discussed in Chapter 1, "From Dorm Room to Boardroom: The Growth of Social Networks," when you set up your account.

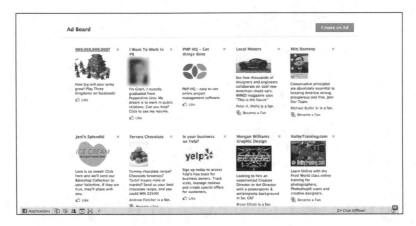

Figure 5.1 The Ad Board displaying the different ads that I have been targeted for. To see all your Ad Board, select the option to see more ads in the right sidebar of your profile.

Throughout this chapter, I talk about common reasons for rejections, a step-by-step guide to create an ad, how to measure your campaigns, and creative ways in which you can use the advertising platform.

Common Reasons for an Ad to be Rejected

Before we walk through the steps to creating a Facebook ad, it is useful to consider the common reasons that your ad could be rejected. Make sure that you don't use any of these tactics and your ad should pass with flying colors.

According to Facebook, the following are the 12 most common reasons for an ad to be rejected:

1. **Capitalization of every word:** Capitalizing every word can give you an unfair advantage over the ads that are running. Also, it is not proper grammar.

2. **Capitalization of entire words:** One of the easiest ways to scream "SPAM" to your target audience is with the capitalization of entire

words. We've all seen these messages before. Admit it; you're usually, if not always, turned off by messages such as LEARN HOW TO IMPROVE YOUR SALARY. Even if the message is useful to you, the capitalization of every word makes it appears spammy.

3. **Incorrect grammar, spelling, and slang:** Do yourself a favor and use proper grammar and spelling. Don't use slang. You and your company will not be viewed as professional if you're not using proper grammar and spelling. Take time to proofread your ad before submitting it to Facebook for review.

4. **Inaccurate ad text:** Facebook is likely to reject ads that do not clearly state the company name, product, or offer.

5. **Deceptive discounts and offers:** This should fall under the "don't be dumb" rule, but unfortunately there are people who try to deceive by making one offer that attracts users, and then giving them something totally different when they click it. This will surely get your ad tossed by Facebook and it will also damage your online reputation.

6. **Irrelevant or inappropriate images:** Only use images that are relevant to your ad. Also, make sure your images are clean. Similar to deceptive discounts, don't be dumb. Help to ensure Facebook is a safe and fun place for people to hang out.

7. **Inappropriate targeting:** Why would you want to spend money targeting one group while speaking to another? Target those that you want your ad to reach. Bottom line.

8. **Destination:** Facebook has developed some particular guidelines when it comes to where you can send your audience. Per Facebook: "All users must be sent to the same landing page when the ad is clicked. The destination may not include fake close behavior, pop-ups. Ads may only be directed to a website or iTunes. When linking to iTunes, the text must explicitly say so. Ads may not be directed to any other download such as PDF, PowerPoint, or Word documents."

9. **Sentence structure:** Simple enough: Use complete sentences. Proper grammar, spelling, and sentence structure will make your ad, and therefore your company, appear unprofessional.

10. **Unacceptable language choice:** Language can't be degrading, derogatory, inappropriate, sexual, or profane in any nature.

11. **Incorrect punctuation:** Similar to other areas that we've talked about, this is yet another reason that your ad will make your company appear

unprofessional. Ensure that someone proofreads your ads before sending them to Facebook for review.

12. **Symbols and numbers in place of words:** The sublanguage of speaking in 140 characters (for both text and now Twitter) has changed how
many people word a sentence. Instead of full words such as "for," many
now replace it with the number 4 instead. This is cause for rejection by
Facebook. Don't substitute symbols or numbers for words.

Step-by-Step Guide to Creating an Ad

One of the great aspects of Facebook Ads is that you can easily experiment with
running campaigns on Facebook. Because you can dictate exactly how much you
want to spend, you can test whatever amount of money you feel comfortable experimenting with.

Now that you've decided that you want to experiment with running an ad, it's a
simple process to actually creating and publishing your ad. It takes only four steps
for your ad to appear for your target demographic.

1. Design Your Ad

After you log into Facebook, scroll to the bottom of the page and select the
Advertising link, as shown in Figure 5.2.

Figure 5.2 To create an ad, find the Advertising link at the bottom of the page of your
profile.

This takes you into the advertising platform. From there, choose the Create an Ad
option to reach the ad editor. The first section is where you create your ad. Select

what the destination URL will be for the ad. It can be an external website or landing page, or you can choose to have your ad point to a Facebook Page, Group, or Application. Select the Title, Body Text (up to 135 characters) and upload an image, if you want.

Depending on whether you use cost-per-impressions (CPM) or cost-per-click (CPC), you need to ensure that your ad is designed in a way to maximize your advertising spend to achieve the goal of either pushing the user to a website or for brand awareness. How you design your Facebook ad can greatly affect its success. In line with this, you'll want to ensure that your ad is designed specifically for the audience who you are targeting. The options available in Facebook Ads allow you to focus your attention on that target audience; therefore, your ad should reflect that.

As you select the title and body text of your ad, be careful not to become too wordy. You don't have long to grab your audience's attention; therefore, make it targeted, simple, concise, and to the point. If your goal is to convince users to do *something* such as click the ad to go to an internal or external link, you need to make sure you have a strong call-to-action and that your message directs them to complete that action such as "Click here to register for the event."

 Tip

When developing a call-to-action, make sure that you're direct: Tell your audience exactly what you want them to do.

Using images are like low-hanging fruit online. Images help to convey your message and grab the audience's attention. Don't run an ad without an image. Use your company logo, product shot, or other relevant image. Don't choose an image with text in it, if you can avoid it, because the limit is only 110 pixels wide by 80 pixels tall. (Hint: That's not that big.)

 Tip

Consider using a landing page: When you convince users to stop what they're doing and instead take time to interact with you online, make sure that you direct them to the most relevant landing page. That can be an internal Facebook page such as a Group, Page, or App. If you point your audience to an external website, consider creating a specific landing page for your Facebook ad.

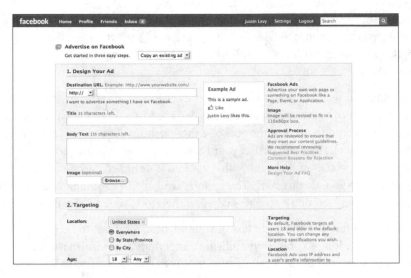

Figure 5.3 As you add elements to your ad, you can preview the results right beside it.

2. Target Your Audience

Decide *whom* you want to target with your ad. Facebook allows you to target based on 11 different filters such as location, age, birthday, sex, keywords, education, and so on (see Figure 5.4).

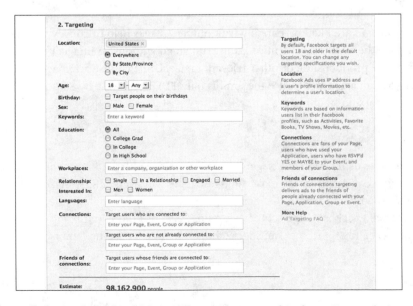

Figure 5.4 Facebook provides 11 different targets to select from. As you design your ad, be sure to spend some time considering these targets.

As you go through these different filters, make sure that you spend quality time thinking about whom you want to target and how the filters can assist in limiting your ad to that specific audience. This is one of the best features within the Facebook Ad platform as compared with Google AdWords. Make sure that you take advantage of this feature and apply the proper filters. For example, if you target people in the Northeast, make sure you apply those filters. Don't just leave the location open to everyone in the United States.

 Tip

> Using keyword targeting can be an extremely powerful way to narrow the size of the potential audience for your ad. Because some of the other targeting options may not limit your search as much as you want or need, keyword targeting can help narrow the search.

As you set different filters, Facebook provides you with an estimate of the number of Facebook users that your ad will reach. For example, if you want to run an ad targeted at 22-year-olds to 27-year-olds who are college graduates and from Massachusetts, Facebook estimates that the ad would have the potential to reach 245,000 (see Figure 5.5).

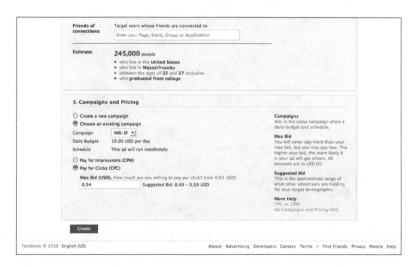

Figure 5.5   By setting your targets, you can view the estimated audience that your ad will have the potential to reach.

The more filters you select, the smaller the population you will reach. Though you may first be inclined to keep your filters more broad so that you'll reach more of the hundreds of millions of people on Facebook, don't follow that first instinct.

The more you focus on advertising, the more the number will decrease. But, you will likely have higher conversion rates because they are focused on your target demographics.

The only issue with targeting is that it is based on the fields that you and others choose to fill in. Therefore, if you don't disclose your location or you have moved without updating your location, the ad estimation tool will be off.

3. Create a Campaign and Set Pricing

After you create your ad and decide *whom* you want to target, the next thing you need to do is to create the actual campaign and set your pricing.

Facebook provides you with the option to set a daily budget and to determine whether you want the ad to run continuously or if you want to target the ad only between certain dates and times (see Figure 5.6). This can be incredibly useful depending on the reason for running the ad. While deciding how much you want to spend daily and what period of time you want the ad to run, you need to choose what you want to pay for.

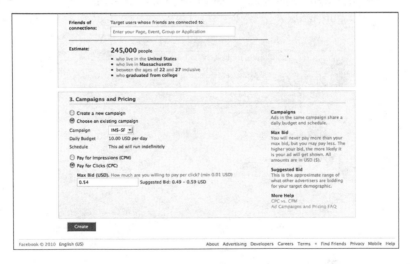

Figure 5.6   Decide what your daily budget is, the schedule for your ad, and whether you want to pay for impressions (CPM) or clicks (CPC).

Facebook allows you to choose between paying per thousand impressions of the ad (CPM) or paying per click on the ad (CPC), as shown in Figure 5.7. Because both options rely on what others are bidding for the same targets, you need to set what your maximum bid is. Facebook tries to help out by providing a suggested bid range based on the other bids it currently has. The decision of how much to bid and whether to go CPM or CPC depends on what your ultimate goals and available budget are.

Figure 5.7   The goals of your ad depend on whether you want to select CPM or CPC. As you can see from the Ad Board, people use Facebook Ads in a variety of ways.

If you try to push users to either an internal or external website and the success will be based on conversions, you probably want to select CPC. You pay per click; therefore, you pay only each time people actually click through. It is then your job to set up that internal or external landing page properly to grab their attention and convert them, based on what your definition of conversion is.

Now, if you want Facebook ads to help with branding and awareness, you can use CPM because what you actually care about is getting your ad in front of as many people as possible.

Whichever option you select, CPC or CPM, be sure to test with both to see how each converts for you.

4. Review and Submit

Now that you've created your ad, you need to review it. When you're satisfied with the ad, choose Place Your Order to submit your ad to Facebook.

Many times advertisers and marketers get caught up so much in the process that they forget about the user experience. To ensure a positive user experience, walk through as a user, from the ad to the landing page. Ask colleagues, friends, or spouses to take a run through the steps and gather their opinions.

After you submit your ad to Facebook, it goes through a quality review to ensure that the ad fits Facebook's quality guidelines. Upon approval of your ad, it will be published according to the targeting and pricing options you selected while creating your ad.

Facebook provides robust analytics about the performance of your campaigns. Use these analytics. Don't ignore them. Dive in and evaluate how your campaign is performing. Rip apart the analytics to gain knowledge and then make necessary changes to ensure that the money you spend is put to its best use.

Analyzing Performance

Facebook provides an excellent reporting tool to gauge the performance of your ad campaign. Analyzing performance is important so that you can make adjustments, not only after your campaign but also during the campaign. By monitoring your performance in real time, or near real time, you can make immediate changes that can turn the tides of a lagging campaign that's only draining your bank account.

When you head into the analytics area, you're immediately greeted with a dashboard where you get an immediate glance at your campaign. From here you can edit your campaign, its status, the daily budget, or duration. You can also see a roll-up report of the major key performance indicators of your campaign including

- Status
- Bid
- Type (CPC or CPM)
- Clicks
- Impressions
- CTR % (Click-through rate)
- Avg. CPC
- Avg. CPM
- Amount Spent

You can see this immediate information for all campaigns you may be running or have run in the past.

Below that dashboard, you can also view a few different graphs for a campaign based on either clicks, impressions, or CTR. Both the dashboard and graphs are a great way to receive an immediate overview of how the campaign is going, and it can help to raise any red flags that may need deeper attention (see Figure 5.8).

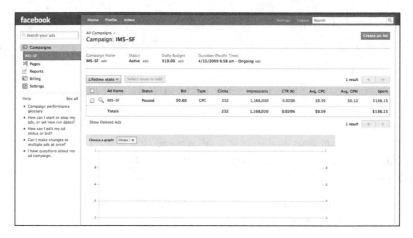

Figure 5.8   There are many different reports that you can run to dig into your campaigns. This enables you to identify trends on-the-fly and make adjustments.

Additionally, Facebook provides three campaign reports:

- **Advertising Performance:** This is the same data provided on the dashboard, but it allows you to apply a few filters and export the data.

- **Responder Demographics:** This report provides demographic data thus allowing you to see who is actually clicking on your ads. This allows you to adjust targets or optimize text or to understand who is attracted to your ads. Again, this information can be filtered and exported.

- **Responder Profiles:** This report, according to Facebook, "provides information about the types of users who see or click on your ads based on interests that they have listed in their personal Facebook profiles."

Through the use of the three reports that Facebook provides and the main dashboard, you can measure and adjust your campaigns on-the-fly, thus making better use of the money that you invest and allowing you to hit your target audiences in a more effective manner.

Summary

It may seem easy to understand why or how you want to use Facebook ads as part of your marketing campaign; however, you can use Facebook ads in several different ways. Let's review just a few of them:

- Product launches

- Webinars

- Recruitment

- Branding/awareness

- Event marketing

- Social good campaigns

Although each uses the same basic elements, they can have different impacts depending on what your goal is. If several of these concepts fit with your company, you should experiment with them to see which seem to resonate with your target audience.

As you can see, there are many uses for Facebook Ads that can integrate into your current online marketing strategy.

Similar to other features around Facebook, the advertising platform will continue to evolve with new features and improved analytics. Until then, use this as a guide to navigate the Facebook Ads platform and begin experimenting. Try CPC versus CPM, A/B test ads with the same targets, adjusting target audiences, and monitoring all your activity.

When used properly, Facebook Ads can be a powerful tool.

6

Extending the Experience with Facebook Apps

Welcome to Facebook Applications. If you're a smart-phone user, especially an iPhone user, you understand the obsession over applications right now. Facebook boasts more than 45,000 applications and continues to grow at a rapid rate. Entire companies are formed around the development of Facebook applications. Companies such as Zynga (shown in Figure 6.1), a social gaming company who also produces games for other social networks such as MySpace, has received $219 million in funding and is now valued at, according to the New York Times, to be at least $1.5 billion and possibly as high as $3 billion.

With all these applications and a growing number of companies competing for your attention, how can this be valuable to you? As a marketer, you can install applications that extend your Facebook profile or Page in a number of ways.

For the most part, any application that you can think of that you would want to share with your personal or professional networks are available in the Application Directory, Facebook's library of applications (see Figure 6.2).

Figure 6.1   Zynga, one of the most popular social gaming companies.

Figure 6.2   Welcome to the Facebook Application Directory.

If you haven't set up an application before, follow along and step into the wild jungle of applications.

Shareability of Applications

As a marketer, one of the most appealing functions about applications is the variety of notifications. Enabling notifications that post status updates to users' Walls helps to spread the application quickly through the network. It extends the number of eyeballs seeing the application nearly instantly. However, users have grown frustrated with application notifications because of how many they receive, especially if they have large networks. And thus, the dilemma over the shareability functionality of applications begins.

Facebook applications usually contain many ways in which they spread virally throughout the network to the 400 million potential users. The best at it utilize every notification option available to applications. Notifications include updates to your Wall as you interact with the application and prompts to refer the application to your network. Both of these open the application up to millions of new people nearly instantly. But, for those applications that are frequently updated, it can become annoying as streams fill with application notifications instead of updates from friends or from Pages they're fans of.

Finding Facebook Applications and Navigating the Directory

To start adding applications to your personal profile or company Page, head over to the Application Directory. You can find this by navigating to the bottom-left portion of your screen and selecting the option under the Applications menu to Browse More Applications, as shown in Figure 6.3).

Figure 6.3   The Facebook Applications menu accessible via the bottom of your browsing window.

When the Application Directory loads, you are greeted with a few options in the center, main column, as shown in Figure 6.4:

- Featured by Facebook

- Applications You May Like

- Recent Activity from Friends

Figure 6.4   The Application Directory Dashboard provides featured by, suggestions, and recent activity by your friends to help suggest new applications to you.

If you haven't gotten lost navigating into one of those applications, you can start finding applications that suit your needs for either your profile or Page by using the menus in the left sidebar. There are a number of ways in which you can start finding applications. Facebook organizes the Application Directory sidebar in the following way:

- Search

- All Applications (see Figure 6.5)

- On Facebook

- External Websites

- Desktop

- Mobile

- Pages

- Prototypes

Figure 6.5 An example of the Education category under All Applications.

Each of these menus allows you to narrow your search by selecting a specific category such as Business, Education, Entertainment, Lifestyle (as shown in Figure 6.6), Sports, Utilities, and more. When you select a category, the Application Directory will load the center, main column with applications that fit that category broken into the groupings previously mentioned (Featured by Facebook, Applications You May Like, and Recent Activity by Friends).

Figure 6.6 There are many categories to choose from. This is the Lifestyle dashboard.

Take some time to navigate to the various categories or run a few searches for applications that you think may be fun, interesting, or helpful to you. Of the more than 44,000+ applications available, you can find at least a few that you'll want to use. An easy way to start is by searching for applications that you're already using on your smartphone (iPhone, Blackberry, Droid, Nexus One, and so on), other social networks, or websites that you log into frequently. Chances are there's an app that will either match exactly or replicate what you want to do (see Figure 6.7).

Figure 6.7 Common applications such as Google Reader and Delicious are available to connect with Facebook via their applications.

Reviewing and Adding an Application

When you find an application that you think may be helpful for you to install, head over to the application so that you can install it and adjust the application's settings. When you select an application, you are first brought to the application's Page where you have an option to go over to the actual application and install it. Similar to the Page you may already be administering or planning on creating, an application Page has all the information about the application including reviews from the community, the number of monthly and active users, and a variety of other information (see Figure 6.8).

Figure 6.8 One of the most popular movie applications, Flixster, has a Facebook profile that provides reviews, the number of monthly and active users, and a lot of other information to help you decide whether you want to download.

When you decide that you want to install an application, head over to the actual application. At this point you are prompted to allow the application to be installed along with a standard Facebook warning, shown in Figure 6.9:

> "Allowing [Application Name] will let it pull your profile information, photos, your friends' info, and other content that it requires to work."

Figure 6.9   The warning message presented every time you choose to install an application.

After the application has been installed, you are usually taken to a Facebook landing page for that application. For example, Flixster (flixster.com), a popular movie rating website, has a robust landing page with multiple tabs of content including the ability to access your Settings menu (see Figure 6.10). The Flixster Settings menu

Figure 6.10   Flixster provides a robust page where you can interact with the application, settings, and your Flixster account info.

provides you with many options to control the notifications and privacy settings of the application. Because Flixster also offers smartphone applications and an external website, there are options to log in to your preexisting account or to create an account. Not all applications have these options, but as more mainstream applications translate to Facebook, similar options will be available.

At this point, you need to add the application to your profile. You usually have a few different choices of where you want the application added to your profile (see Figure 6.11):

- Wall

- Boxes tab

- Tab

Figure 6.11   The option to add the application to different areas on your profile.

Be careful when deciding where to add your application. You don't want to overcrowd your personal profile or Facebook Page with too many applications. Another warning: Be careful of the number of notifications you have turned on for your applications. While in the marketer's mindset you can understand why it's such a great idea to have notifications turned on; you can quickly figure out the issue of that having too many applications posting too many notifications into your stream. See Figures 6.12 and 6.13 for a clean profile and a crowded profile.

Figure 6.12   An example of a clean profile with only a couple applications strategically placed.

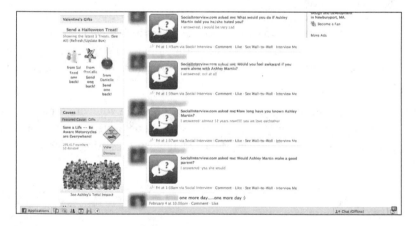

Figure 6.13   An example of a busy, crowded profile that doesn't lend itself to interaction.

Managing Your Applications

Now that you have installed a few applications, you occasionally need to manage them. From time to time you should remove an application or edit another application's settings. How you manage your applications depend on if you need to make adjustments to those installed on your personal profile or on your Facebook Page.

If you want to manage your personal applications, open the Applications menu on the bottom navigation bar. From this expanded menu you can view your most recently used applications, access your bookmarked applications, or choose Edit Your Applications to start managing all your installed applications.

After the dashboard loads, you have a few different options to help you find the application that you want to edit:

- Recently Used

- Bookmarked

- Added to Profile

- Authorized

- Allowed to Post

- Granted Additional Permissions

- Facebook Prototypes

Each application allows you the option to edit its settings, view its profile page, or remove the application from your profile. Although viewing the profile page and removing an application are self-explanatory, let's explore what the settings menu contains.

Although the Flixster settings that we discussed provided you with tons of options to manage what types of Flixster notifications would be posted to your Wall, the settings available in these menus are standard application settings. They offer the following options:

- Ability to Add a Box

- Privacy Options

  - Everyone

  - Friends and Networks

  - Friends of Friends

  - Only Friends

  - Only Me

  - Customize

- Bookmark

- Additional Permissions

If you want to manage your Facebook Page applications, navigate to the Page that you want to edit. When you're there, select the option to edit your page. In the Page editor, you have direct access to the applications that you have installed onto the Page.

Creating Your Own Facebook Application

Although this book does not cover how to write a Facebook application, if you're interested, there are plenty of companies available online to help bring your concept to reality. You might use a basic knowledge of coding to write a simple application, but for anything for your company, definitely consider hiring a firm to build your Facebook application.

Installing the Developer Application

The first step to creating your application is to install another application. Yep. You need to install the Developer application that allows you to create new applications, as shown in Figure 6.14.

Figure 6.14   The Developer application portal filled with all sorts of news and updates.

After the Developer application is installed, this will be your portal into updates from Facebook, the status of open issues, and stats on any of your applications. Besides this information, Facebook also providers developers with a special forum where they can get together and help each other out, as shown in Figure 6.15.

Figure 6.15 The Facebook Platform Developer Forum.

Completing the Application Configuration Form

To start creating your application, the first step is to create a name for your new app and agree to the Facebook Terms. Although we're all used to just skipping past terms and conditions, it is worth it to actually review the Facebook Terms. Facebook heavily enforces its terms; the last thing you want is to have the world's largest social network mad at you.

After naming your application, you see the application configuration form in Figure 6.16 where you can tweak all the settings for your application. These settings are broken up into seven categories, which have several options to fill in under each category:

Figure 6.16 The Application Configuration Form.

- Basic

- Authentication

- Profiles

- Canvas

- Connect

- Widgets

- Advanced

Although it may seem that these options have been covered ad naseum, it is these settings that make or break your application in many ways. If not set up properly, even if you have an excellent application, it won't matter.

After spending time going through all these settings, you need to add your application code and then submit it to the Application Directory.

While this is, admittedly, not an exhaustive guide to developing and launching a Facebook application, it does provide you with the framework from which you can get started with the process. If you need a more extensive guide to developing a Facebook application, there are many titles available that will help guide you.

Summary

Facebook applications can help you customize your friends' or fans' experiences when visiting your Profile or Page. Facebook apps can help you aggregate content from around the Internet into a central area, provide games for your friends or fans to interact with, or other possibilities. Take some time to explore Facebook applications and see if there are any that may be useful to you, your company, or your community. If you have specific ideas for an application that you think may be useful, explore developing your own Facebook application. However, as you begin to add and develop applications, be cognizant of how crowded you may be making your Profile or Page, especially your Wall since many of the applications provide frequent updates.

Addressing Privacy Concerns

Throughout this book, you have been encouraged to take advantage of the many features available in Facebook. Knowing that you've been a good student and took your notes you've now filled in your city, state, phone number, marital status, uploaded photos, tagged videos, and linked your notes together. The marketer side of you perked up and created a Page and/or Group, linked that to your profile, and did a lot of that same stuff over there, too. Maybe you thought about the amount of personal and professional information you're sharing. Maybe not. Maybe you have taken the time to review the Terms of Service and Privacy Policy. But, chances are, like every other Terms of Service or Privacy Policy, you haven't bothered to look. Have you thought of the ways in which these policies can affect your ability to market your brand, product, or service? Have you considered where all that information that you share is disappearing to? Can Google and the other search engines see all that information? Should you keep your personal account separate from these marketing activities? Can you even do that? These are all questions that fly around the interwebs when discussing privacy concerns and Facebook.

As Facebook continues to grow, it is becoming less and less a purely personal network. It's not the network you go to just to relax at the end of the day and catch up with a few friends or check out family photos. Nowadays many people use Facebook as part of their online reputation management and personal/professional branding strategy. People use Facebook for both personal and professional connections and networking. As Facebook grows larger and people continue to blur the line between personal and professional, concerns over privacy continue to arise.

Privacy within Facebook needs to be addressed on multiple levels:

- The sharing of personal information and whether, because of that, you should use Facebook as a professional tool as well.

- How to properly configure the privacy settings for both your personal profile and any Pages or Groups you administer and manage.

- What the Terms of Service and Privacy Policy actually allow you to do within Facebook.

- How all this ties together and affects marketers trying to use Facebook as part of their marketing strategy for their brand, product, or service.

All these issues will be addressed throughout the next few pages.

The Two Faces of Privacy on Facebook

With Facebook starting out as a personal network, it has been a hard transition for people to become used to it as also a professional network. Most use LinkedIn as a professional network, Facebook as a personal network, and Twitter is a hybrid that people are still trying to figure out. But with the growth rate of Facebook, many have started to turn to it as a personal branding tool and professional network. Marketers have begun turning to Facebook with Facebook Pages, Groups, and advertisements as a way to reach out to their prospects, customers, and fans.

This transition has created a dilemma for many folks because they are resistant to using Facebook as a professional network, yet their colleagues, competition, and companies are becoming active on the network. Also, as we develop friends in our industries, we want to extend that friendship and therefore turn to Facebook. This starts to blur that line even further between work and home. However, as Dawn Foster of *WebWorkerDaily* points out, we don't want to confuse "personal" for "private":

> You can actually be professional and personal at the same time in social media without too much effort. When we talk about 'being personal' on social media websites, I think that many people confuse 'personal' with 'private.' The reality is that you get to decide what to share

and what not to share, so you can still keep most areas of your private life private.[1]

To deal with this dilemma, individuals typically have three options to choose from:

1. Maintain a single Facebook profile that combines personal and professional.

2. Maintain two different Facebook profiles: one personal and one professional.

3. Keeping Facebook only personal and not mixing work into it.

Each one of these has both upsides and downsides with not one clear answer or best practice, as of yet. Though it might not be clear yet, this will be important for you as a marketer or company. Let's explore each of these options.

Single Facebook Profile

If you don't mind mixing personal and professional, you can maintain a single Facebook profile in which all engagement with the platform originates from that one profile. This enables people to get to know the real you. It's just like the two faces that most wear on a daily basis: the way you are at your office and the way you are at home, with friends, or family.

Although so many of us are used to this split personality, why should we act like this? Why can't we be the same person at work as we are at home, maybe just dressed up a little nicer? You have the same likes and dislikes, the same problems and victories, and your family, friends, enemies, colleagues, and competitors don't change when you're at work versus when you're at home (see Figure 7.1).

Furthermore, realizing its growth, Facebook has continued to add features that allow you to tweak your privacy settings to allow you to use a single profile but limit access to data sets based on permissions, lists, and rules that you set up. This means that you can create a list of your colleagues and then deny that list access to certain aspects of your profile. By setting this up properly, you can achieve the privacy and separation that you want while not having to bother with two separate profiles or avoiding Facebook as a professional network.

---

[1] http://webworkerdaily.com/2010/01/11/private-or-personal-in-social-media/

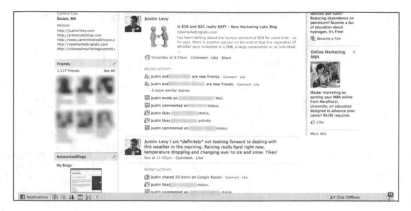

Figure 7.1 Mixing professional promotion and personal thoughts, I use my Facebook profile for a blend of professional and personal uses.

Two Different Facebook Profiles

If you want to maintain split personas, between your personal and professional lives, you can create two different Facebook profiles. One Facebook profile you can create as your personal account in which you upload personal photos, videos, and bio info. This is the account where you interact with your friends, family, and others that you allow into your personal circle. Just remember to use a personal email account and not one that anyone in your professional life knows. If you do use the same email, you open your personal profile to being found by colleagues. Of course, you can always ignore the friend request, but it is much easier and simpler to just use a separate email account.

The second account should be set up under a work email address that your colleagues would use to search for you. Under this profile you can upload any professional content that you would like to share. To reduce confusion between these two profiles, you should consider hiding one of the profiles from Facebook searches and indexing by search engines. (This can be done through the privacy settings for your profile.) Which one to hide is up to you, or you can hide both, if you want.

Not Mixing Personal and Work

Your last option is to simply not mix personal and work. Some people decide that the easiest route is just not to promote their presence on Facebook. They maintain Facebook as their personal social network and use LinkedIn as their professional network to connect with colleagues, as shown in Figure 7.2. For those wanting to maintain that separation between personal and work, you might find this to be your cleanest option.

Figure 7.2   Some choose to maintain their personal presence on Facebook and their corporate/professional presence on LinkedIn. Brad chooses to use Facebook as a personal social network while staying active in other professional networks.

Privacy Settings

Understanding and tweaking the privacy settings for both personal profiles and for any Pages and Groups you manage is important. Otherwise, you might expose, share, or allow others to share information about you or your brand that you don't want shared, at least not without your permission.

Although it's not one of the most fun things to do within Facebook, you need to take some time and walk through each of the settings discussed.

Personal Privacy Settings

If you haven't done so already, spend some time going through the privacy settings and configuring based on your comfort with exposing personal information or other data and to whom you want to expose that information to.

To begin configuring your privacy settings, roll over the Settings link in the top navigation. One of the options under the drop-down menu will be for Privacy Settings. After you select the Privacy Settings option, you see a main privacy settings area in which you can control the privacy settings surrounding the following (see Figure 7.3):

- **Profile Information:** Control who can see your profile and who can post to your Wall.

- **Contact Information:** Allow you to control who can contact you on Facebook and who can see your contact information including your email.

Figure 7.3 An overview of the various personal privacy settings that can be adjusted based on desired level of openness.

- **Applications and Websites:** Control what information is available to Facebook-enhanced applications and websites.

- **Search:** Tweak who can see the search result for your profile, not only in Facebook search results, but also in search engines.

- **Block List:** Control who can interact with you on Facebook.

Digging into the Profile Information, you can gain control over the following aspects of your profile, as shown in Figure 7.4:

- About Me

- Personal Info

- Birthday

Figure 7.4 Some of the many options available under the Profile Information selection within the personal privacy settings.

- Religious and Political Views

- Family and Relationship

- Education and Work

- Photos and Videos of Me

- Photo Albums

- Posts by Me

- Allow Friends to Post on my Wall

- Posts by Friends

- Comments on Posts

For each of these options, you have the ability to set exactly who can see and inter-act with this data (see Figure 7.5). Your options are

- Everyone

- Friends and Networks

- Friends of Friends

- Only Friends

- Customize

If you choose the Customize option, you can limit the visibility of that information to only

- Friends of Friends
- Only Friends

- Specific People
- Only Yourself

Figure 7.5 For most of the privacy settings, you have the ability to limit or grant access based on a few permission levels.

Under the Customize option, as shown in Figure 7.6, you also can choose to hide the information from specific people.

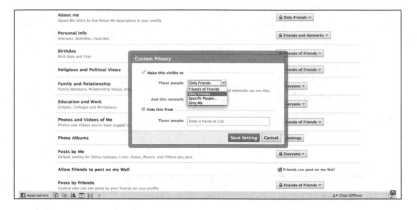

Figure 7.6 The Customize privacy setting allows you to customize specific people or networks that you want to have access to a specific segment of information.

These same visibility options are available for all the preceding options under the Profile Information, including, and for some, what is most important, Photos. Photos carries its own set of options that allow you to control the level of access per photo album. Of all control options, the ability to control who can see what photos and who has the capabilities to tag you in photos, always seems to be the option that the community, especially the professional community, cares most about (see Figure 7.7).

Figure 7.7 Under the Photos setting, you can grant or limit access to specific photo albums.

Similar to the Profile Information settings, the Contact Information selection allows for all the same visibility control options for the following areas (see Figure 7.8):

- IM Screen Name
- Mobile Phone
- Other Phone
- Current Address
- Website

- Hometown
- Add Me as a Friend
- Send Me a Message
- Email Address

Figure 7.8   The Contact Information option controls access to your personal information such as phone, address, website, email, and more.

Between the Profile Information and Contact Information settings, you can control the visibility options to your entire profile. But as we have learned throughout this book, the power of Facebook isn't just in what you can do within the walls of Facebook, but what you can interact with outside of Facebook using your profile, Facebook Connect, and applications. For this reason, Facebook allows you to control the privacy settings surrounding applications and websites that communicate with Facebook using your profile information, as shown in Figure 7.9. Under these settings you're able to control

- What you Share
- What Your Friends Can Share About You—information such as your birthday, videos, photos, shared links, hometown, education, and other profile data
- Blocked Applications
- Ignore Application Invites

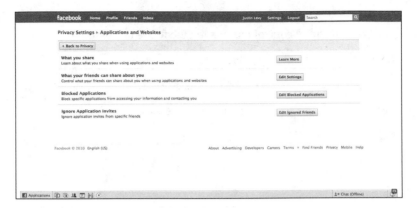

Figure 7.9   As the ability to use your Facebook profile around the Internet through Facebook Connect continues, you can control the available level of access, permissions, and options.

Although the preceding options are important to control valuable pieces of information, the exposure of your profile to search engines in 2007 drove a lot of controversy. It drove so much controversy that it prompted Facebook to issue the following privacy announcement concerning the update, as shown in Figure 7.10:

> Worried about search engines? Your information is safe. There have been misleading rumors recently about Facebook indexing all of your information on Google. This is not true. Facebook created public search listings in 2007 to enable people to search for your name and see a link to your Facebook profile. They will only see a basic set of information.

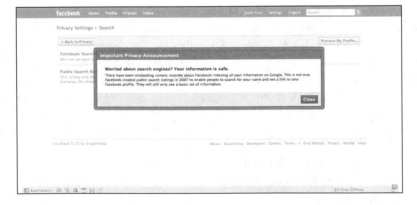

Figure 7.10   When accessing the Search privacy settings, Facebook presents you with a prompt providing you with information about your profile and its exposure to search engines.

With that being said, Facebook allows you to turn on or off the visibility of your profile to search engines. It should be noted that if you do allow your profile to be visible to search engines, the search engines will index all information within your profile that you mark as available to Everyone.

Besides the ability to control visibility to public search engines, you can also control the visibility of your profile to Facebook search results. The same settings that are available under the Profile Information and Contract Information settings are also available for the Facebook Search Results privacy settings (see Figure 7.11).

Finally, under the privacy Settings, you can block people by profile name and email, as shown in Figure 7.12.

Figure 7.11   You can control your profile's visibility to Facebook search results and to public search engines.

Figure 7.12   Is there someone that you don't want to find you on Facebook, but you don't want to restrict your profile to everyone? Under the Block settings, you can block people based on profile name and email.

So why is it so important to ensure that you carefully go through all these settings? Well, if you consider what we previously discussed about the potential option to maintain both your personal and professional lives from the same profile, you might want the ability to control who can see what. Additionally, you can control the ability of others to tag photos or videos of you and write on your Wall because if you don't it is possible that even if you choose not to upload pictures or videos from a holiday party or weekend night out, someone else can, and they can tag you in them. Whether you did anything wrong isn't the only reason to be concerned. You might just want to simply control what aspects of your personal life that your colleagues can see and vice versa.

As a marketer you need to pay special attention to the choice to expose data to public search engines. As we reviewed, any information marked as available to "Everyone" will be indexed by search engines. This can be important for gaining a few extra links for your company through exposing your, and your staff, work information on your personal profiles. Also, if you're an independent or freelance marketer or trying to position yourself for the next big jump, you might want to expose particular aspects of your profile so that recruiters running background searches, general searches, or doing research can find you among those results.

However, it's not only the privacy settings that you can control that are important, but also the Privacy Policies and Terms of Services that Facebook implements for its users. These policies can have a profound affect on how you use Facebook for yourself and your company, product, or service.

Pages Privacy Settings

Now that you've spent some time adjusting the privacy settings of your personal profile, it is time to turn your attention to your Facebook Page. Although the number of settings to be adjusted and tweaked isn't as many as those available in the personal profile settings, we still want to walk through and understand the available settings and how they might be used. You need to focus on only two settings, as shown in Figure 7.13.

To start, head over to your Facebook Page and click Edit Page. This takes you to the Page editor where you can tweak a number of settings and adjust what appears in boxes or tabs, the permissions, and a number of other options to help you customize your Page. As it pertains to privacy, though, we focus solely on the Settings and Wall Settings options.

For the Settings option, you can

- Restrict people from certain countries, which you can specify, from viewing the Page.

Figure 7.13   Adjusting privacy or access options under Pages is controlled by two primary settings under the Page editor: Settings and Wall Settings.

- Set age restrictions, thus preventing certain age groups from accessing the Page. These age restriction options are

  - Anyone (13+)
  - People over 19
  - People over 17
  - People over 21
  - People over 18
  - Alcohol related

- You also can choose whether the Page is published. If the Page isn't in a "published" status, no one else, except for admins, can see the Page. Therefore, the Page should not be published if you're only working on setting it up for the first time or you're making major updates to the Page (see Figure 7.14).

Figure 7.14   The ability to restrict based on country, age, and whether the Page is published or not can all be found under the Settings option in the Page editor.

The next set of options that we need to consider is the Wall Settings options. These settings include some basic options for deciding which tab is the default landing tab, the default view of the Wall, and whether comments on stories can be expanded. Also a set of fan permissions allow you to control fans' ability to post on the Wall. If posting on the Page Wall by fans is allowed, a subset of permissions allows you to control whether they can also post photos, videos, or links to the Wall, as shown in Figure 7.15.

Figure 7.15   Under the Wall Settings, you can adjust some basic options for the way the Page behaves and a detailed set of fan permissions.

Some brands limit the ability of fans to write or post content on their Walls. Although, in general, writing on the Wall shouldn't pose any issues, it is understandable that allowing anyone to post photos, videos, or links could cause a moderation issue. If you put the time into moderating and actively managing the Wall posts, you might as well leave it open to the community; however, if persistent issues with content posted occur, at least you know that the ability exists to limit one or all these permissions (see Figures 7.16 and 7.17).

Figure 7.16   Hip-hop superstar, P. Diddy, doesn't allow fans to interact with his Page in any way: no comments, photos, videos, or links.

Figure 7.17   Coca-Cola allows fans to leave Wall comments, post photos, links, and videos. This increases community development and openness.

Group Privacy Settings

The privacy settings available to Group admins are the same as those available to Page admins except the way the actual options are laid out is slightly different. The one exception is that within Groups, you can control the visibility of the Group (as shown in Figure 7.18). Your options are

- **Open:** The Group is completely open. Anyone can join and search engines indexed by the Group.

- **Closed:** The Group appears in Facebook search results. Only the Group description is visible unless you're a member. Admins must approve all requests to join the Group.

- **Secret:** The Group is completely hidden from all search results and does not appear in members' profiles. Membership is by invitation only.

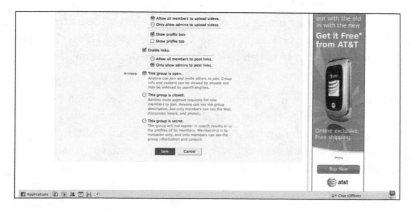

Figure 7.18   Groups allow you to control the visibility of the entire group to Facebook search results and to public search engines.

As you can see, as Facebook has grown, it implemented many privacy settings to allow you to control how others can interact with you and your brand.

Facebook's Privacy Policy

As with any large social network, Facebook has developed, and continues to iterate, a set of policies that are the guiding rules of the network. The privacy policies and terms of services are put into place as a way to govern the large social network.

When Facebook originally started out, the network was private. Essentially all information was opt-in only. To view any information other than some basic data points and a bio picture, you had to be "friended" by the individual to see other information. But, over time, Facebook tweaked the platform and eventually moved toward a more open network. Information was still all opt-in, but these updates allowed users the option of whether they wanted to expose some, or all, of their information to Facebook search results and external search engines. In a January 2010 interview, CEO and founder Mark Zuckerberg talked about the battle between openness and privacy. During a speech at the Crunchie awards, Zuckerberg stated:

> "People have really gotten comfortable not only sharing more informa-
> tion and different kinds, but more openly and with more people. That
> social norm is just something that has evolved over time...in the last 5
> or 6 years, blogging has taken off in a huge way, and just all these dif-
> ferent services that have people sharing all this information."[2]

Although a lot of controversy over this speech occurred, you need to not lose sight of what Zuckerberg and his executive team deal with at Facebook. Facebook, in terms of population, is one of the largest countries in the world. Therefore, Zuckerberg and his team need to implement strategies and policies that they think will be best for all the citizens of Facebook. Sometimes these aren't the popular decisions, but most of the time, they are done to help better the entire network. That will cause some percentage of people to become upset. This is the same thing that happens in any country when new laws are passed or existing laws are updated.

One example of trying to do the right thing for the entire community was during a major round of updates to the privacy policy during December 2009 when Facebook released a major update and change to its privacy policies. The goal was to give users more granular control over their privacy settings by, among other updates, allowing them to select, on a per-post basis, who can see content posted to

[2] http://www.guardian.co.uk/technology/2010/jan/11/facebook-privacy

their Facebook profile. Also, Facebook announced that it was removing regional networks. When Facebook was originally created, it included having to choose a network, such as a country, state, city, college, work, or other related groups. The concept behind this was that it would make it easier to connect with people in that group, and also only those within the group could see your profile without being friends with you. This had the reverse effect when Facebook began growing at exponential rates. People became part of large networks, sometimes into the millions. This, of course, made privacy a mute point. So, in this December 2009 update, Facebook tried to change these issues. To help even further, Facebook provided a suggested privacy level for you that you could accept or tweak.

In an open letter to the entire network, Zuckerberg explained:

> "We're adding something that many of you have asked for—the ability to control who sees each individual piece of content you create or upload.... We've worked hard to build controls that we think will be better for you, but we also understand that everyone's needs are different. We'll suggest settings for you based on your current level of privacy...."[3]

Immediately after this open letter was posted and the updates flowed in, revolt from the community started. The claim was that by creating these updates, though you could restrict your activities more, it actually tended to lend people to sharing more. Eventually, this calmed down, and people adapted to the new privacy policies and options.

Again, as with a large country, decisions are made and laws or guidelines are created that are put into place for the overall benefit or protection of the community. Not everyone will like these changes, and for some, it could, occasionally, restrict what they're doing.

Summary

Even though Facebook tries to ensure that you have the controls necessary to control your privacy, you should always be careful of the amount of information you share, not only on Facebook, but also on the Internet, in general. Although Facebook can provide you many tools that can be beneficial to not only yourself, but also to your company, you should only engage at a level that you ultimately feel comfortable with.

---

[3] http://blog.facebook.com/blog.php?post=190423927130

8

Developing a Facebook Marketing Strategy

Throughout the book, we have spent time discussing specific features of Facebook and how they may be implemented into your professional life. Much of what we discussed is beneficial for your personal and professional presence on Facebook. Although the individual features can be beneficial, Facebook becomes extremely successful if you can tie all these features together.

Now that you have a clearer understanding of the available feature set, we now have to design a comprehensive strategy for you to follow when you get to the final page of this book. One blanket strategy will not be the answer because you can use Facebook in a variety of different ways. More important, your company's needs are different than the next company that reads this. Your product or service is different. Your prospect and customers are different. Your goals and success metrics are different.

Throughout this chapter, we discuss a couple different strategies along with a set of actionable tips for each strategy. Before we can dive into different strategies, we need to lay out a set of questions for you to answer to help frame the strategies and select which is the best for you to start with. Take a few minutes to answer the following questions:

1. Why do you want to use Facebook for your business?

2. What are the specific goals you want to achieve for your business with Facebook?

3. How can you use Facebook to fill a need, want, or void that your prospects or customers are experiencing with your company or your competitors?

4. Are you currently doing any online advertising? If so, would you like it if you could target those ads more appropriately?

5. How do you plan on measuring success?

Now that you've answered those questions, it is easier to know which stack of tips to start conquering. At the end of the day, all strategies mentioned throughout this book will more than likely be helpful to you at some point. So, having a working knowledge, or at least, understanding, of how to use this social network overall is beneficial.

Boiled down, Facebook can be used the most effectively by businesses in three main ways:

1. **Community building:** You need to deploy a community building strategy if your main goal is to develop a strong overall presence on Facebook. You may already be engaging on other social networks, especially those in which you can interact in real time with your prospects, customers, or fans. Using Facebook for community building enables you to use the most tools available within Facebook. Your overall goal is to generate conversations, drive awareness, increase your fan base, and be an active part in this community. No community is ever successful without a strong community manager. Be prepared to play this role or delegate it to someone within your organization.

2. **Marketing and promotion:** Although through the building of a community you have the opportunity to market and promote your products, services, or upcoming events, if that is all that you truly care about, you need to start focusing your time and attention on some tools first. Using Facebook as a marketing and promotional tool can be useful in driving traffic to landing pages or event registration or in promoting awareness around a product launch or special offer.

3. **Advertising:** A straight advertising strategy through Facebook is the most limited strategy of the three; however, some organizations want to use Facebook only as another advertising stream for their company, product, or service. This is okay but you will not be harnessing the true power of Facebook. Tools are in place, as we have previously discussed, that enable you to solely advertise through Facebook. If that's what you're looking for, skip forward a few pages and pick up your reading at the start of this strategy.

These strategies and the tools to execute these strategies often cross over, as shown in Figure 8.1.

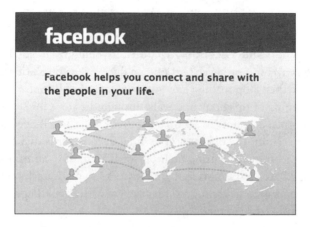

Figure 8.1   The social web connects us with no borders. Developing and executing upon a strategy is important to provide guidance on best practices, how to engage, and several other factors.

You could select one of these strategies to begin using or you could integrate all three of them into your digital marketing plan. Additionally, you can probably think of a few other strategies that could be used to fold Facebook into your marketing plan. Either way, the most important thing is that you realize that Facebook can be a beneficial addition to your current marketing plan and that you recognize that the social network can be used in a variety of ways that can help your business.

Let's start by exploring the more broad but potentially most powerful strategy: using Facebook to build community.

Designing a Community Building Strategy

Okay—so you've decided that you want to use Facebook to build community. That's great! The hard part is over. But, you have managed to choose the strategy that is the hardest to develop and demands that you keep up with it on a constant basis. The cost to implement: hours and hours of sweat equity. However, using Facebook for community building will allow you to apply the many, hopefully helpful, principles that we've discussed throughout the course of this book.

Building a community in Facebook will allow you to increase brand awareness, build community, drive conversations, market and promote your brand, products, and services. With Facebook growing at mind blowing rates, it is becoming more and more likely that your prospects and customers will be hanging out in Facebook.

But, now you need to know how you're going to build that community. You're eager to get going and instead of listening to a bunch of pontification, you just want to get up and running. Let's start with five tactical steps that you can do as soon as you're done reading:

1. **Create a personal Facebook account:** If you don't already have a Facebook account or haven't set one up during the course of reading this book, then stop reading and go to www.facebook.com. Go back to the beginning of this book and walk through the steps for setting up your personal account. To set up a Facebook Page, you'll need to have a personal account to hook it to. One thing to consider is that some people feel uncomfortable using their personal account to administer Facebook Pages or Groups that are for work. If you do feel uncomfortable, set up a second account to manage your Facebook Pages or Groups from (see Figure 8.2).

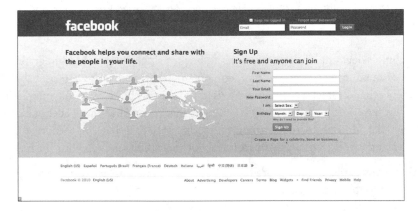

Figure 8.2 To sign up for a Facebook account, it is as simple as filling in a few field boxes.

Tip

Setting up a second account to manage corporate Facebook Pages or Groups can make it easier to keep personal and professional lives separated. That way, if you leave your company or someone else takes over the community management of your company's Facebook presence, it is as easy as giving the new person the credentials to the second account. There are no ties to your personal account.

2. **Create a Facebook Page or Group for your business:** We've gone over the differences between a Facebook Page or Group. You need to decide which is better for your goals, but suffice it to say, if you want to build a public community, go the route of Pages. Head back to Chapter 3, "Establishing a Corporate Presence," and follow the steps outlined to set up your Facebook Page. When you create your Facebook Page, make sure you add photos, videos, biographical information, your website, and any other relevant information to complete your Facebook Page. If you decide to use a Facebook Group, spend time going through all the features available and tweaking appropriately. Before you start inviting people to your community, make sure that everything is set up. Remember, when your prospects and customers start finding you on Facebook, it will be another point of impression for them. Therefore, put your best foot forward and take the time to set up your Facebook Page or Group properly (see Figures 8.3 and 8.4).

Figure 8.3 A Facebook Page serves as a "human profile" for businesses, celebrities, politicians, and a number of other folks.

Figure 8.4 A Facebook Group is a great way to create a private community.

3. **Let your current community know:** If you're already active on other social networks, you can use these networks to invite people to join your Facebook Page or Group. Depending on whether you have colleagues who you are friends with under your personal account, you could also post a status update on your personal account inviting and encouraging people to fan your Page or Group, as shown in Figure 8.5.

Figure 8.5 Sending a message to your community on other networks is a great way to alert your followers or fans that you've also got a presence on Facebook.

4. **Add your Facebook presence into your marketing creatives:** Unless you're a technology or social media-focused company, you're probably using many other methods to connect with your prospects

and customers outside of social networks. Therefore, you need to inform all of them about your newly created Facebook presence. One of the easiest ways to accomplish this is to start adding it into all your marketing creatives such as your newsletters, brochures, billboards, digital advertising, website, and any other areas where you might provide contact information (see Figure 8.6).

Figure 8.6   Promoting your Facebook presence on your website is one example of incorporating FB into your other marketing creatives.

5. **Add your Facebook Page to email signatures, business cards, and other areas in which you provide other forms of contact information,** as shown in Figure 8.7. One of the simplest ways to start letting others know you're now active on Facebook is by adding a call-to-action to connect with your Facebook Page or Group on your email signatures, business cards, and any other areas in which you encourage people to contact you. Think about how many emails you send per day. Many of us send 25 to 50 or even 100 to 200 (if you're an email addict) emails per day. That adds up to a lot of opportunities to provide your contacts with an opportunity to connect with you.

In addition to these options, you can encourage your community to connect with you on Facebook in several other ways. Utilize these as appropriate.

As you develop a stronger presence and build a larger community on Facebook, you need to test, measure, test, measure, repeat, to find out what works best for your community. Some communities engage with shared articles. Others prefer to respond to questions asking for input. While other individuals may want an area, such as a discussion forum, in which they can go to engage. Be sure to test these

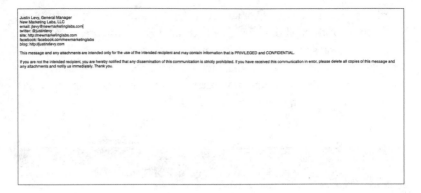

Figure 8.7   One way to grow your Facebook subscribers is to include your Facebook Page or Group in your email signature.

different engagement methods so that you will know the best way to continually build a stronger and more engaged community (see Figure 8.8).

Figure 8.8   *The New Community Rules* is a book that utilizes a Facebook Page to share relevant stories with the community.

Designing a Promotions Strategy

One of the more targeted ways that you can successfully use Facebook as part of your overall marketing plan is to use it for promoting events, products, services, or special offers. Utilizing Facebook Pages, Ads, and the Events capabilities, Facebook can be used to promote in multiple different ways. Looking for some ideas of how you can use Facebook in this way? Check out these ideas:

- Promote your upcoming webinar by creating an event and posting it to your personal Wall and your Pages Wall. Send an email to everyone in

your personal and corporate network on Facebook encouraging them
to attend.

- Use the Photos section of your Facebook Page to leak out photos of an
  upcoming product to your fans.

- Throwing a party or meetup at an upcoming conference? Run a
  Facebook Ad for the targeted positions and demographic. Couple this
  with an Event listing.

- Promote a new service via a Note on your Facebook Page. If several
  people were involved with the project, tag everyone who helped out.
  This can help to spread the message by alerting them and posting the
  tagged note to their personal Wall depending on their privacy settings.

- Create a Facebook app and run it from your Facebook Page to create an
  experience for your fans (think: *Fight Club*, www.welcometofc.com) by
  utilizing Facebook Connect and enable social sharing capabilities, thus
  increasing the visibility of that product and your Facebook Page.

Your ability to successfully use Facebook as a promotions vehicle is limited only to
your imagination. The most obvious promotions will be those that require an RSVP
because that has a perfect fit with the Events section of Facebook Pages. Those can
be easily coupled with a Facebook ad. But, there are several other ways, as previously
highlighted, that you can use Facebook to promote an upcoming event, product
launch, new service, or other news that you want to increase awareness of (see
Figure 8.9).

Figure 8.9 An example of an offline event promoted on Facebook to help increase
awareness and serve as an RSVP for the event.

Designing an Advertising Strategy

Similar to the promotions strategy, using Facebook to augment your advertising strategy can be another targeted method to integrating Facebook into your overall marketing plan. Some ideas for how you can use Facebook Ads are

- Advertise an upcoming webinar.

- Advertise an upcoming offline event such as a conference, party, or meetup.

- Advertise a product launch, new service offering, or other special offer.

- Use Facebook Ads as a recruiting tool to advertise a new position.

- Advertise your Facebook Page or Group to encourage more subscribers.

One of the benefits of Facebook Ads is that you can test with a small spend. If it is successful, you can easily renew the campaign or decide to tweak it and then relaunch it.

Make sure you follow the tips provided in Chapter 5, "Facebook Advertising: How and Why You Should Be Using It," to ensure that your ad stands out among the other three to four ads that display along with your ad in the right sidebar (see Figure 8.10).

Figure 8.10   To create an ad on Facebook, it is as simple as filling in the fields. There is always a preview of the ad that is created.

The Importance of Measurement

It doesn't matter which strategy you decide is appropriate to implement if it is the right strategy for you and your company. What is important is to ensure that you measure your activity. You need ways to figure out if your chosen strategy is successful for your needs. Facebook provides several ways to measure your engagement on the network depending on which strategy you deploy.

Facebook Insights

If you're going to use a Facebook Page to build community, be sure to use the Insights functionality, as shown in Figure 8.11.

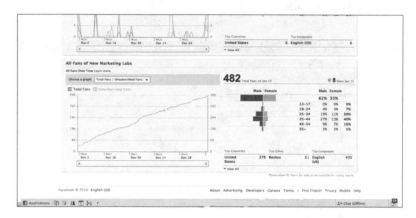

Figure 8.11   Facebook Insights allows you to run comparison reporting that allows the administrators to track trends over a period of time.

Facebook Insights provides the Page administrators with a number of data points, including

- The number of posts/updates that you've had on your Page.
- The number of interactions that your community has had on your Page.
- The number of interactions per post.
- An approximated score on post quality.
- The number of discussion posts.
- The number of reviews.
- The number of mentions.
- How many new fans have come onboard.
- How many new fans have subscribed in the past week.
- How many fans have unsubscribed.

- The breakout between male and female.

- The breakout between age groups.

- A graph of your friends based on country and language.

- The number of page views that your Page has received.

In addition to just raw numbers, Facebook provides the administrators with several different graphs, grids, and other interesting forms of content under the Insights section of a Facebook Page, as shown in Figure 8.12.

Figure 8.12   Facebook Insights provides the administrators of the Facebook Page with in-depth analysis focused on interactions and demographics.

Using Facebook Insights is the primary tool to judge what type of content is right for your community. Not only can you monitor how well different types of content perform, but you can also make certain judgments about the types of content you may share based on demographics. You can also use Facebook Insights to ensure that you're staying consistent with your status updates and sharing. With busy marketers' and executives' schedules, it is easy to forget to engage on Facebook.

Facebook Advertising

Besides providing a great platform for targeted advertising, the Facebook Ad platform provides a robust set of analytics (see Figure 8.13).

Facebook Ads allows you to measure the performance of your advertising campaign by providing you with the following data points:

- Current bid

- Type of ad—either cost-per-click or cost-per-impression

Figure 8.13   Facebook makes it easy to create an Ad directly from a Facebook Page. Alternatively, on a personal page you can click Create an Ad on the right sidebar.

- Number of clicks

- Number of impressions

- Click-through rate

- Average cost-per-click or cost per-impression

- Average CPM

- Your total spend to date on the ad

 Tip

Confused about what bids, cost-per-click, cost-per-impression, and everything else previously listed are? Flip back to Chapter 5 for an in-depth overview of these features.

Facebook also allows you to run three different types of reports:

1. Advertising Performance

2. Responder Demographics

3. Responder Profiles

All these reports can be summarized by account, campaign, or ad and can be run based on daily, weekly, monthly, or custom time frames, as shown in Figure 8.14.

Facebook Ads has an option to tell you the size of your potential target demographic. Although this feature isn't expressly called out as a feature by Facebook, you can find the data by selecting the option to create a new ad. After you get into

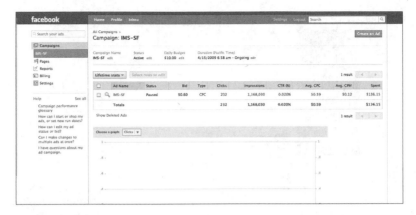

Figure 8.14 Facebook offers a comprehensive Ad dashboard from which you can dig down into ads that you're currently executing and run a variety of reports.

the first screen, you can select the options for your target demographic. Facebook then tells you how many users fit that demographic. You can then cancel the option to create an ad or continue moving forward with the customization of your ad.

This can be a great way to see if your target demographic is even on Facebook and if it is, then what its approximate size is.

Web Analytics

As you spend more time engaging in Facebook and pushing prospects, customers, and fans from Facebook to different websites or landing pages, you need to ensure that you measure your referrer traffic to see where Facebook ranks. This provides you with a pulse on whether people are actually doing anything with the information you provide in Facebook. Although you may have a lot of interaction taking place within Facebook, if your goal is to push that traffic to an external website or landing page, you need to give attention to your web analytics package, such as Google Analytics. Depending on your other digital marketing efforts, it is not surprising to usually see Facebook in the Top 5 for referring traffic especially if you're active. If you notice that Facebook is not ranking in the Top 5, you should take a closer look at how well you convert folks from Facebook to that external website or landing page, as shown in Figure 8.15.

 Tip

You can measure Facebook Page performance with Google Analytics, but it will take a few extra steps to make them talk to each other nicely. For the detailed list, visit: http://www.webdigi.co.uk/blog/2010/google-analytics-for-facebook-fan-pages/.

Site Usage	Goal Set 1							Views:				
Visits		**Pages/Visit**		**Avg. Time on Site**		**% New Visits**		**Bounce Rate**				
775		**1.60**		**00:01:31**		**74.45%**		**73.03%**				
% of Site Total: 39.95%		Site Avg: 1.53 (4.20%)		Site Avg: 00:01:20 (13.73%)		Site Avg: 77.58% (-4.03%)		Site Avg: 77.16% (-5.36%)				

	Source	None	Visits ↓	Pages/Visit	Avg. Time on Site	% New Visits	Bounce Rate
1.	twitter.com		296	1.62	00:02:00	80.41%	73.65%
2.	facebook.com		74	1.82	00:02:21	66.22%	66.22%
3.	chrisbrogan.com		57	1.74	00:02:10	68.42%	68.42%
4.	google.com		55	1.47	00:01:22	54.55%	67.27%
5.	images.google.com		31	2.03	00:00:11	100.00%	77.42%
6.	hootsuite.com		25	1.36	00:01:02	64.00%	68.00%
7.	newmarketinglabs.com		21	2.14	00:02:37	80.95%	42.86%
8.	lmodules.com		17	1.00	00:00:00	17.65%	100.00%
9.	friendfeed.com		15	1.47	00:00:44	73.33%	66.67%
10.	centernetworks.com		14	1.00	00:00:00	92.86%	100.00%

| Filter Source: | containing | | Go | Advanced Filter | | Go to: 1 | Show rows: 10 | 1 - 10 of 92 |

Figure 8.15   Make sure that you constantly check to see where Facebook ranks in your referrer traffic.

Marketing Software

If you use a marketing software such as HubSpot, an inbound marketing software that allows you to track your online marketing and lead generation efforts, you can take your external traffic one step further. With software packages such as HubSpot, you can actually measure the traffic originating in Facebook, leaving and headed to your external website or landing page and then converting on a lead generation form for a webinar that you may be running. If this is integrated with your CRM system, something such as Salesforce.com, you can follow that lead now through the sales pipeline to a closed deal. Apply estimated hours and salary spent on this entire process, and you quickly have your return on investment (ROI) on your hard and soft expenses on Facebook (see Figure 8.16).

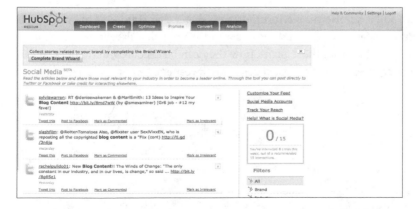

Figure 8.16   HubSpot is an inbound marketing software that provides small-to-medium businesses with a marketing dashboard that easily allows them to track social media into the sales funnel.

Other Measuring Methods

If you're still not finding the data that you need, you can always export the relevant statistics and dump them into a spreadsheet program such as Microsoft Excel, Google Docs, or Apple Numbers, as shown in Figure 8.17. That way you can develop more complex graphs, track trends, and apply other numbers such as manpower investment to help you determine the ROI of your spend in Facebook. Remember that, unless you use Facebook Ads, your engagement in Facebook doesn't have hard costs associated with it; however, a lot of sweat equity will go into keeping your Pages, Groups, and Ads running properly. This is a cost that you need to measure.

Facebook Activity										
		Fans				Activity (Status Updates)				
	Current	Weekly Change	Monthly Change	Monthly Goal	% to Goal	Current	Weekly Change	Monthly Change	Goal	% to Goal
GoToMeeting	326					4				
GoToWebinar	51					2				
GoToAssist	67					1				
GoToMyPC	288					1				
GoView	58					0				
HiDefConference	27					1				
Workshifting	169					2				
Workshifting Blog Activity										

Figure 8.17   Use a spreadsheet to track goals and trends and manipulate your Facebook Insights analytics even deeper.

Summary

As we discussed throughout this book, you can use Facebook in many ways to enhance your marketing programs. The tools are, in general, the same. It's dependent on *how* you decide to use the tools provided that determine the impact you may see as a result of your efforts. For this reason you need to determine your strategy using the questions provided at the beginning of this chapter to help guide your engagement on Facebook.

Facebook is a powerful platform for a marketer that continues to grow and add new features. Therefore you must understand the ways that Facebook can be used, what strategies align with those plans, how they can be executed, and how you can measure your investment, both hard costs and sweat equity.

 Tip

Looking for additional Facebook strategies, lists of tactical approaches, case studies, and information on measurement? Check out these blogs, all of which provide massive amounts of information about Facebook:

- AllFacebook.com

- InsideFacebook.com

- Mashable.com

Even if a particular strategy fits your needs now, such as the advertising strategy, be sure to check back and see if developing a community or using Facebook to help you promote or market your product or service may be helpful to your organization. New and innovative case studies continue to come out all the time about how to use Facebook in new and creative ways to market, promote, advertise, and build community.

9

Using Facebook to Develop Communities

At a basic level, Facebook represents one large community. Within that large community a limitless number of subcommunities form. People form communities around their interests, hobbies, events, companies, products, services, celebrities, schools, or even favorite foods. We form and use these communities in the same manner that we would in the physical world. We engage with one another, form bonds, share interesting articles, upload photos and videos, and invite others with similar interests to join our communities.

Although forums are still a popular way for these communities to form, they have graduated into more developed community platforms. Some communities choose to build premium communities.

Although these enterprise level premium communities offer expanded features and more customization, they're also expensive and more suited for larger companies and organizations. Also, because these premium communities are set up on a different domain or a subdomain of your website, you then have to work harder to bring people to the party.

Facebook serves this purpose perfectly. Facebook has a large pond from which users can fish for others with similar interests or hobbies. As discussed in Chapter 3, "Establishing a Corporate Presence," you need to decide between a Page or Group when figuring out what features will be needed for your community or what your specific preferences are. But, no matter which you choose, you can quickly and easily set up a community, for free, on Facebook.

When the community is set up, you should search for other similar Pages and Groups and begin engaging there as well. Don't be spammy about it, but you'll slowly gain users over into your community the more you engage in the other communities and demonstrate a passion, knowledge, and presence.

Another benefit of using Facebook to set up communities, either using a Page or Group, is that it offers greater reach by breaking down geographic walls. Of course, some physical communities grow large enough that they break into multiple chapters with localized community groups all over the world. But, those groups still remain local, and although some larger organizational bylaws may exist to help guide the local organization, they form their own separate and unique communities as well.

With Facebook it's not necessary to separate into localized communities, unless the users decide that is what is best for them. Instead, they can all interact and benefit from one another.

As you build your community, you need to decide on who will be your community manager. Ideally, this person should be either you or someone from your team. As the community manager you need to give your community reasons to keep coming back. All of us nowadays have too many things competing for our attention. Those that tend to get our attention will be the items that stay top of mind and that we find interesting, helpful, useful, or otherwise needed. Therefore, to continue to grow an active and growing community on Facebook, you need to engage your community; however, you can't just engage them by simply updating your Page or Group status every day. You need to provide content in different formats because all members of your community will demand to receive their information and content in different ways. Some of us prefer video whereas others love photos, and some may want thought-provoking links to read.

Let's explore some of the different types of communities that can be formed on Facebook, how users are utilizing them, and along the way, some tips to help you maximize engagement within your community.

Building a Community for Your Company, Product, or Service

Due to the growing size of Facebook, more and more of your prospects and customers are on Facebook; therefore, you should not ignore Facebook as a viable way to form a community. Even if you have created an enterprise-level, private community, you should still ensure that your brand is properly represented on Facebook. As discussed in Chapter 3, you can use Facebook to create a Page (see Figure 9.1) or Group around your company, product, or service. This serves as your main presence on Facebook and as another outpost from which you can communicate and connect with your prospects, customers, or fans.

Figure 9.1 Coca-Cola's Facebook page.

Developing an active community around your company, product, or service on Facebook can be beneficial, especially if you are successful at encouraging conversations. How can this engagement be so successful on Facebook? To start, every time a community member interacts on your Page, either by uploading a photo or video, leaving a Wall post, commenting on a status update, or pressing the Like button, Facebook can filter that interaction to the top of the news feed on the home page for other "fans" of your Page and the specific user's feed. If there is consistent interaction, you can stay top of mind, at least on Facebook, with your prospects, customers, or fans. If you couple that with regular ads and the addition of new content within Facebook and other areas around the interwebs, you'll be on your way to developing a strong online brand.

An example of a company that exemplifies the use of Facebook for branding and interaction is HubSpot, shown in Figure 9.2. HubSpot is a Cambridge, MA-based company that makes an inbound marketing software that helps businesses "get found." As of November 2009 HubSpot had more 7,500 fans. Although the number alone is impressive, simply having a large number of fans or followers doesn't mean anything. However, HubSpot doesn't just have a large following, they have a large and engaged following. HubSpot regularly posts a range of different information to its Facebook Page. On any given status update, HubSpot receives a dozen or more Likes and an equal number of comments. HubSpot also has an active Discussions area and utilizes the Events, Video, and several other features extensively.

Figure 9.2   HubSpot, a Cambridge, MA-based inbound marketing software company, which utilizes Facebook extensively to build a community around its brand.

To provide consistent and diversified content can become harder and harder as you go along. When you first set up your community on Facebook you'll think of all kinds of information to share. But, as time goes on, you might find yourself struggling to provide a consistent flow of information. Here are a few suggestions to help you continue to engage with your community and provide a consistent flow of content.

Upload Photos

Do you have product or software photographs or screenshots that you can share? Create albums for each of your products or different sections of your software and upload your photos and screenshots (see Figure 9.3). Other ideas include

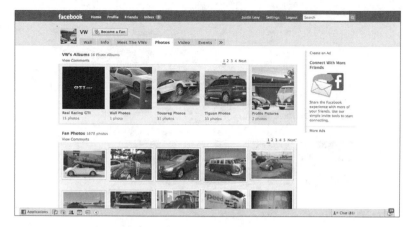

Figure 9.3   VW uploads photos of its different vehicles. It also allows fans of the Page to upload photos.

- Upload photos of your team at work.

- Create a photo tour of your office.

- Take photos of events you might sponsor, speak at, or participate in.

Upload Videos

You can use the video functionality within Facebook to provide various content. Video is a great form of media to ensure you utilize it not only on Facebook but also across the interwebs. Video allows your community to create a bond with you because it can connect with a human face. Instead of always relying on the written word, a podcast, or a still photo, a video shows life.

If you have a product or software, try creating a short demo, or series of demos, showcasing a specific feature (see Figure 9.4). Other ideas include

- If you take your team out for happy hour, bring along a camcorder and shoot short videos of your team having fun together.

- Upload customer testimonials.

- Shoot quick snippets from your team and create a video thanking your customers for their business.

- Record interviews with people from your industry and upload those interviews. Link the video to a full-text version of the interview elsewhere.

If you don't like either of those ideas, try allowing your customers to submit questions either via Facebook or another form of communications. Compile all those

Figure 9.4   At my restaurant, Caminito Argentinean Steakhouse, we regularly upload instructional videos as part of our Prime Cuts TV series.

questions and create a frequently asked questions video. Upload that into Facebook; then you can point people to that video when they have a question. If there are a lot of questions, maybe you could organize them into categories and create multiple videos. In the description for the video, you might include a link where the viewer could go to read the text version of the answer.

Ask Questions

One of the easiest and most basic ways to trigger people to interact with you, especially on Facebook, is to simply ask a question (see Figure 9.5). Because the status update will drop into the live news feed, it is easy for others to quickly leave an answer. As more people continue to engage, the status update will keep floating back to the top of the stream. If you jump in and start interacting as well, you'll create a nice discussion based around something as simple as a status update.

Figure 9.5   Boston.com regularly asks questions to engage with its community.

So, what kind of questions are you supposed to ask? Ask anything. Ask your community how they're doing today. Pose a question with a link to an article in your industry. Ask for feedback on something you're working on. Whatever the question is, make sure it is about your community and not you. Make them feel like they're part of the community.

RSS

Do you have a corporate or industry blog that you and your team write regularly on? Pull that RSS feed into your community, either via the Notes section or one of the many RSS applications available (see Figure 9.6). Many companies also use a RSS feed on their corporate news and media sections. By pulling in your corporate news or media sections, this can provide your community with updates on your company and make it easier on you because it will be automated.

Figure 9.6   Digital Dads, a blog dedicated to being a resource for dads, ports its RSS feed using the Notes feature. A regular engagement on each post differs from the interaction on the Digital Dads blog.

Provide Exclusives

Is there something that you could share with your community on Facebook that isn't shared any place else yet? If you have a medium-to-strong community, try announcing a new product, software release, or company news via Facebook first. If your community figures out that you're likely to release company information via Facebook, it will continually check in and be an active part of the community.

These are just a few ideas of a limitless list of ways that you could create various pieces of content to keep your community engaged. The most important aspect of keeping your community engaged around your company, product, or service is to figure out what your community wants and needs to get from spending its precious time on your Facebook Page or Group. Then provide it that level of engagement and type of content repeatedly and consistently.

Consistently check in with your community to see if you're providing them what they want. When you do decide to experiment, measure success by tracking the engagement.

Building an Internal Community

Facebook provides the opportunity for you to use Groups to form private communities. This is great for companies that may have distributed workers or a growing workforce and wants to have a common area for its team to hang out and engage with one another. Large corporations tend to have private enterprise level communities built for them using a professional community platform. But companies that don't need a lot of features, or may not have budget for an expensive platform, can turn to Facebook to fill that communications void.

Many corporations have realized that their employees are all on Facebook and already spend a lot of time interacting on the platform. So, instead of forcing them to log in to yet another website, they decide to use Facebook as an internal communications platform for their community (see Figure 9.7).

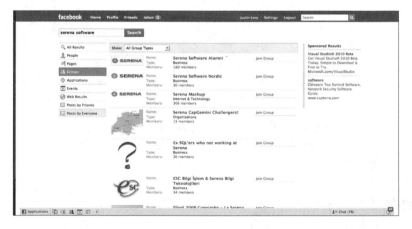

Figure 9.7   Serena Software uses several different Facebook Groups as part of their "intranet."

One of the downsides to using Facebook instead of a private community is that although the Group can be private, you don't control the data. With that said, heed caution when sharing anything private or proprietary. You don't control the data and are not privy to decisions that Facebook may make concerning the platform, therefore you wouldn't want to wake up one day to find out that Facebook decided to make Groups completely public, thus disclosing confidential data that could be detrimental to your company and a benefit to your competition. If you have those needs, you're best suited to contact one of the many private enterprise-level community platforms.

Using Facebook as a Focus Group

Continuing with the concept of using Facebook as a private community for your company, what about creating a Group as a private focus group for your company, product, or service?

Using a Group, you could invite in a select group of your prospects or customers and use it as a platform to ask for candid feedback, provide demos, and open access to certain groups or individuals within your company or shots of upcoming products or software releases. Again, remember, don't show anything you're worried about leaking out. Though, if you're engaged in any type of blogger or PR relations, that is a risk you always run into when showing early releases of a product or software version.

As Facebook continues to grow at a rapid rate, it becomes one of the most attractive properties on the Internet to form a community. Although the ability to form a community around something such as an interest, hobby, company, or celebrity seems natural, social media, of which Facebook is a major part of, provides us a different type of opportunity.

Building a Personal Community

Facebook offers us the ability to build our own personal communities. These communities are built around us and not a hobby, interest, or other subject that we are the community manager of. Most of the time these personal communities form on the user's personal profile; however, when these communities grow to be large, the user needs to create a Page to avoid hitting friending limitations set by Facebook. Either way, these communities can grow to be larger and more powerful than a traditional organization at times. How is this possible? The social web allows us to become, as Chris Brogan and Julien Smith coined, "trust agents." Brogan and Smith define trust agents as

> "[D]igital savvy people who use the Web to humanize businesses using transparency, honesty, and genuine relationships. As a result, they wield enough online influence to build up or bring down a business's reputation.... In an online world defined by transparency, becoming a trust agent is no easy task, but once you've established your reputation, you can build influence, share it, and reap the benefits of it for your business. When you've learned a trust agent's secrets, your words carry more

power and more weight than any PR firm or big corporate marketing department."

Therefore, using many of the tips that have been provided here and throughout the rest of this book can be useful for personal profiles as well. As you build your corporate online brand, it is important to be building your online personal brand as well.

What are some ways that you can develop strong personal, or for that matter, professional communities?

Be Helpful

One of the easiest ways to begin building a strong community is to be as helpful as possible, as often as possible (see Figure 9.8). Be a resource for your community. By providing help to your community on a regular basis, they can begin coming to you with questions. Your community can also begin to recommend you to others because of your resourcefulness, and that can allow your community to continue to grow larger and tighter.

Figure 9.8   Regularly sharing interesting links from around the web is one way of being helpful to your community.

Connect Often

Connectoften with the greater community. You can do this by commenting on other's statuses or sending a private message if you know someone is having a rough day. Make sure you note people's birthdays and use that as an easy way to connect with them on their special day. Go through other's pictures and videos and leave comments. If you realize that you haven't reached out to someone in a while, make sure you stop by and say hi.

You'd be surprised how much impact you can have on the larger community by just being there and connecting. This can become even truer as your personal community begins developing into a larger community. People will notice that you're connecting often both with your community and the larger community that is Facebook.

Be a Connector

While you're busy connecting often with the members of your community, be a connector as much as possible as well (see Figure 9.9). Are there two people who you think could mutually benefit by you connecting them? Send them a message introducing them. As Chris Brogan has described it to me many times in the past, you want to be at the "elbow of every deal." By playing that elbow role, you're being helpful and connecting with members of your community. At the same time, you're building up equity because those people that you connect with will remember you forming that connection for them. That doesn't mean that they owe you a favor per se. But, you'll find the more often you try to be helpful by being considered a connector, the more goodwill and similar situations will come your way.

Figure 9.9   Amber is a natural connector. Amber focuses her attention on being helpful and connecting others all over the web, not only just on Facebook.

Use Lists

Using the list feature within Facebook can help you to create small communities for yourself based on interests, location, school, work, or anything else you want to create a list around (see Figure 9.10). Although this won't help to build a community in the sense that you invite people into a private area where you connect, it can help you to connect often with members of your personal community. By setting up lists and checking in with those lists often, it can help to make a growing personal community more manageable. It can also help you to organize your personal community around the many different segments of your life.

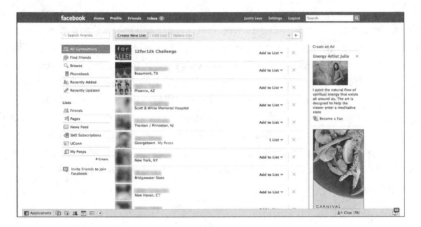

Figure 9.10   Make use of the Lists feature for helping to categorize your friends. Suggestions for lists include by school, work, interest, or geographic location.

This can help you to segment your sharing of information, especially if you have a wide range of tastes. For instance, you might be a foodie and therefore you like to share recipes, interesting articles, discuss TV food shows, and leave status updates about the different restaurants you visit. You might decide that this information wouldn't be of interest to those that you work with. By adding those members of your community who are foodies, you'll ensure that you're only sharing that content with them. For your foodie community, they will appreciate the targeted information even if they don't realize that you have created a foodie list.

Although all these suggestions can help you to grow a community, develop relationships, build influence and reputation, you need to ensure that everything you're doing is genuine. Please don't be fake in trying to grow a community. Don't do it for the numbers or for the perceived power that you might develop. It ruins people's trust and doesn't bode as a positive strategy for you personally or professionally or that of your company.

Business Benefit from Personal Communities

Although it might not seem like it, the building of personal communities can also be beneficial for business. This book is not meant to focus on personal branding. That's not why you're taking the time to read it. There are plenty of other books that address the benefits of personal branding using online tools; however, it does matter to touch on it for just a moment as it relates to businesses benefiting from large personal communities.

Businesses can benefit from employees that have large personal communities on Facebook. How? Because if you're fostering a great company culture where your employees enjoy where they work and what they work on, then they're more likely to want to share interesting projects they're working on, product releases, or other company news. If they have a large community formed on Facebook, or any other social network for that matter, they're likely to turn to that community to share that information. With a few keystrokes they have the potential to send more conversations about the news and more traffic to your website then, sometimes, a press release could. Even if on a pure numbers basis it does not send more traffic, it will potentially be more targeted traffic and conversations. That employee has built up trust with his community and by being human and sharing what matters to them, in this case, their work, the employee is also helping to humanize their business.

Having an employee that has a strong personal community can be more powerful, at times, than a company presence on Facebook. Therefore, it makes sense to foster and encourage employee engagement on Facebook.

When deciding to set up a community on Facebook, you should keep in mind what type of community you want to set up. You can set up a Facebook Page around your brand, as HubSpot has successfully done, or you could set up your Page around your industry, as Wine Searcher has done. Both have their benefits, and you may choose to build out both communities. There is no right or wrong answer here. Both have their benefits.

Building a Community Around a Hobby or Interest

Another way to develop a community on any platform, including Facebook, is around a hobby or special interest. These niche communities have been around for years. Many of us have probably spent time on a forum board doing research or engaging in a topic that was of interest to us. These topics can range from a love for vehicles, music, exercise, a city, or just about anything else you can think of. People tend to belong to multiple groups in their personal and professional lives; therefore, online communities serve as great areas for them to stay engaged with others.

An example of highly engaged communities based around an interest or hobby are the wine communities formed on Facebook. There are no shortage of Pages dedicated to the celebration and discussion of wine. One in particular definitely serves as a learning lesson for others to follow. As shown in Figure 9.11, the Wine Page (URL) is created by Wine Searcher (www.wine-searcher.com) and claims to be the largest and most used independent search engine for wine. Instead of creating a community around Wine Searcher, its team decided to create the community around the greater topic of wine. As of November 2009, the Facebook Page has more than 750,000 fans. Any given status update will have hundreds of "Likes" and comments.

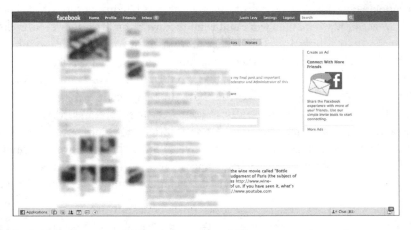

Figure 9.11   The Wine Facebook Page created by Wine Searcher to form a community around the celebration of wine.

As with the development of personal communities, it may seem odd that I've mentioned forming a community around an interest or hobby in a book that is geared towards businesses and, specifically, marketers. But, it really isn't that far off if you think about it.

For every interest or hobby, there are plenty of businesses that support that interest. If you're a foodie, there are restaurants, food television shows, kitchen gadget stores, and cooking classes that you may be involved in or visit often. Does your business support or provide products and services for one of these activities? If so, you could involve yourself with other communities already created on Facebook or you could create your own Page or Group to build a community. Instead of creating it around your product or service, it could be created around the hobby or interest that your company, product, or service provides for. This community wouldn't be used to solely promote your company, product, or service but, instead, to have conversations around the specific industry that your company is involved in.

Summary

Whether you're passionate about being a foodie, a Boston Red Sox fan, a fan of Jay-Z, or a customer of a corporation, there is a Page or Group on Facebook for you. You should also try creating a community around something that matters to you. You'd be amazed at how many others will be interested. Niche communities can grow at crazy rates, especially when the members of the community are as passionate as you are.

Combine the information discussed in Chapter 3 and the information provided here to find yourself a few communities to join on Facebook and create your own. Remember the tips provided and you can move into some of the real benefits of Facebook.

10

Best in Class

Facebook Pages and Groups offer administrators many options to enable them to customize the experience of their users. These features can be utilized in an infinite number of ways. But, are you using these features in the best possible ways?

Although tens of thousands of Pages and Groups are on Facebook, only a select few really stand out from the pack. We're going to focus on the "Best in Class" Pages as Groups tend to be private communities with a limited feature set. The current push is for Groups to transfer over to Pages. Why? Because Pages are public, offer a more diverse feature set, and is the community platform/feature that Facebook has decided to continue developing. By the time you read this book, it is possible that Groups could be a legacy feature and a thing of the past. Therefore, the focus is on Pages.

These Pages are considered the "Best in Class" because they either push the platform to its limits, utilize the Pages in unique and interesting ways, or demonstrate the full use of the tools available.

Volkswagen

Volkswagen (VW) stepped out and away from the pack when it launched its Pages. VW created individual Pages for each of its vehicles (a total of 14 to date) and then rolled those up to a corporate VW page. VW took the, at the time, newly released, FBML capabilities and extended its corporate Page in a customized way (see Figure 10.1).

Figure 10.1   Landing tab for the VW Facebook Page.

Upon landing on the VW page (www.facebook.com/vw), the user can "Meet the VWs." Each vehicle line is represented by a tile on the landing page. If you click one of these tiles, you are then kicked over to that vehicle's Page.

On this same landing page, VW also added in a Facebook application (see Figure 10.2) that analyzes "you" by sucking in all the information you enter into your profile and based on that information, it recommends a VW vehicle that it believes will be best suited for you. How cool is that!?!

Elsewhere on the VW corporate Page you can find tons of photos and videos that have been uploaded and an active Events tab that shows all upcoming VW events. VW also encourages fans to upload their own photos and videos as a way of extending the community. As of March 2010, this community had grown to more than 349,000 fans. These fans are passionate and engaged on the Wall of the VW page.

Each individual vehicle line Page has, depending on the popularity of the vehicle, upward of tens of thousands of fans that actively upload photos, videos, and post to the pages Wall. Each vehicle line Page also contains a customized advertisement for the vehicle that if clicked brings you over to the VW website and onto that specific vehicle page where you can learn more information, see pricing, and contact a dealer (see Figure 10.3).

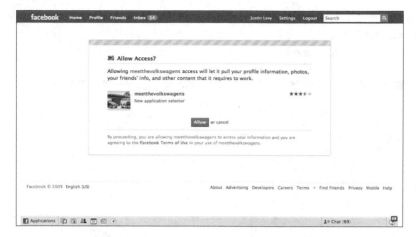

Figure 10.2   The VW "Meet the Volkswagens" analysis application.

Figure 10.3   VW Jetta Facebook Page.

Trust Agents

Trust Agents is a *New York Times* and *Wall Street Journal* best-selling book written by Chris Brogan and Julien Smith published in August 2009. Prior to the launch of the book, Chris and Julien created a Facebook Page as a way to interact with their community and help to combine communities that each of them separately had. It was another outpost to bring more exposure to the book and start conversations around the concepts discussed in the book.

Chris and Julien didn't build out the Page utilizing some of the more custom features as some of our other Best in Class Pages have. But, what they did do was take some of the basic features and use them to build a strong and loyal community. Instead of pumping only in an RSS feed and updating a status from time to time, both Chris and Julien interacted on the Page throughout the day. Within the first couple weeks of the Page being up, Trust Agents had more than 2,000 fans interacting on a regular basis with Chris and Julien. Chris and Julien did their best to respond to every comment they received, as shown in Figure 10.4.

Figure 10.4 *Trust Agents* Facebook Page showing Chris Brogan and Julien Smith actively engaging their community.

Additionally, Chris and Julien produced a lot of content on the *Trust Agents* Page that was exclusive to that page. That's saying a lot about their devotion to the book and to their community because both Chris and Julien generate a lot of other content elsewhere around the Internet.

To be a part of the conversation taking place, you must join the community. It's not as though you can access the information, questions, videos, and notes on Chris' or Julien's personal blogs. On many of the other Pages and Groups that were explored, this wasn't the case. The Page served as a one-way stream of information automatically pushed from other sources.

On any given day you might find a video of Chris and Julien recording the audio version of the book to a member of the community seeding a question about trust. Within minutes there are multiple comments and people "liking" the content. It appears as though both Chris and Julien have developed trust among their fans.

Microsoft Office

In July 2009, the Microsoft Office team launched its Facebook Pages. The Microsoft Office team created individual Pages for each product (Word, PowerPoint, Outlook, and such). Microsoft then rolled all these individual product Pages up into the Microsoft Office Page. It appears that this concept is based on the VW corporate and individual vehicle Pages. But Microsoft Office took the use of the FBML to another level with the sheer amount of content it integrated onto the Pages (see Figure 10.5).

Figure 10.5   Microsoft Office Your Office Facebook Page landing tab with video ribbon and access to the Microsoft Office product Pages.

When you visit the Microsoft Office Page at www.facebook.com/office, you automatically land on a customized Your Office tab. The tab has a ribbon of videos that play based on which product you click in the toolbar. Just below that you can select to head off onto one of the product Pages. If you navigate over to the Tips/Tricks tab (see Figure 10.6), you find a multitude of content on this page. You can check out everything from available templates with previews to daily tips and tons of resources. All these links take you back to the relevant section on the Microsoft Office website.

Figure 10.6   Tips/Tricks tab on Microsoft Office Facebook Page with integrated content, calls-to-action, and more for each Microsoft Office product.

Besides all these features, the Microsoft Office team has also uploaded a ton of videos and has added buttons that will take you to its other social media outposts.

Gary Vaynerchuk

Gary Vaynerchuk has become an Internet phenomenon. Gary Vaynerchuk is the popular owner of Wine Library located in Springfield, New Jersey, the host of the daily online video show Wine Library TV, and is involved in several other projects. Vaynerchuk catapulted his personal brand during 2008–2009 and became one of the most in-demand public speakers in the industry, signed a 10-book deal with Harper Books worth a reported $1,000,000, and was a guest on practically every early morning and late night show on cable television.

Because Facebook has a limitation of 5,000 friends on personal accounts, Gary, like many others with large networks, had to create a Page to continue growing his presence and reach on Facebook. As of March 2010, Gary had more than 41,000 fans and growing (see Figure 10.7).

Figure 10.7 Gary Vaynerchuk's Facebook Page.

Similar to *Trust Agents*, Gary didn't do anything as creative or innovative as VW, Jonas Brothers, or Microsoft Office. But, what Gary has done exceptionally well is use the Page as a way to build a growing community of Vayneriacs, as Gary likes to refer to his fans as.

Gary regularly interacts with fans and answers questions. Gary's fans are very active on the Page and regularly post content, interesting links, questions, and tons of other information.

Gary used the FBML code to extend his Facebook Page somewhat by adding in a tab that contains all his television appearances (see Figure 10.8), a tab that contains other social networks where Gary hangs out, and a tab that allows you to reach out to Gary to work with him on a variety of projects he is involved in. The extra tabs actually aren't any more than an extension of exactly what you can find either on his Wine Library TV site (www.winelibrarytv.com) or his personal blog (www. garyvaynerchuk.com).

Figure 10.8   Gary Vaynerchuk's Gary on TV tab where you can view some of his TV appearances.

Gary uses UStream on a regular basis as a way of connecting in real time with his fans. It will be interesting to see if Gary integrates the UStream application that should be deployed to the masses by the time you read this. This integration would allow Gary to begin interacting with fans right from Facebook instead of needing to tell everyone on Facebook to head over to UStream to chat with him.

Barack Obama

During his presidential campaign, Barack Obama and campaign manger, David Plouffe, turned to social media as a way to reach out to constituents. It allowed Obama to hear the American public's concerns on platforms that they felt comfortable sharing on. Obama's use of social media and his activation of people to help spread the campaign's message is one of the primary ways he was so wildly successful in raising funding and defeating Senator John McCain by a large margin on election day.

One of the primary tools that Obama and his team used was a Facebook Page (www.facebook.com/barackobama), as shown in Figure 10.9. After Obama became the 44th president of the United States, his team continued to turn to using Facebook as a means of communicating directly with the American public. The Facebook Page is *very* active, and there is usually one update or so per day. What is different than on many of the other pages that were chosen as part of the "Best in Class" group is that the Obama Page is closed to allowing fans to publish or share on the Wall. This is expected and sure doesn't come as any surprise to most people. Everyone can still comment on, like, or share any update that the Obama administration publishes, though.

Figure 10.9 United States President Barack Obama's Facebook Page.

As of March 2010, the Page had more than 7.8 million fans and continued to grow. One of the more interesting uses was when President Obama held an online town hall and the White House took questions on a section of the White House site, and then the President selected certain questions to answer during this town hall. Although the online town hall did not take place exclusively on Facebook, the video was posted to Facebook (see Figure 10.10). Overall, the online town hall had 92,937 people who submitted 103,978 questions and cast 1,782,650 votes, according to the White House. On Facebook alone, as of August 2009, there had been more than 5,000 comments and 40,500 users who liked the video.

Figure 10.10 An example of a video posted to the Facebook Page by President Barack Obama's team. This video was of an online town hall that the President conducted.

Although the Page is not necessarily different or innovative—if anything it is more restrictive than other pages—it is interesting to see President Obama and the White

House staff continuing to utilize this as a main source of communicating with the American people directly.

Jonas Brothers

The Jonas Brothers are a musical group that typically appeals to teen girls. With millions of fans around the world, the Jonas Brothers sought out a Facebook Page as one way for them to stay connected.

When you head over to the Jonas Brothers page (www.facebook.com/jonasbrothers), you land on the Boxes tab where they have a vibrant and active Discussion Board. The Jonas Brothers also allow you to listen to their music through a music application and buy their newest single on iTunes (see Figure 10.11).

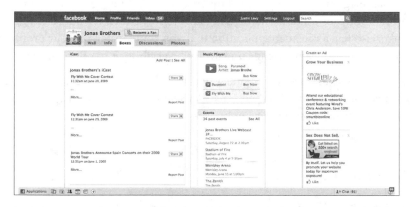

Figure 10.11   Jonas Brothers Facebook Page Landing tab.

The Jonas Brothers upload their music videos and behind-the-scenes videos at concerts, album signings, and other public appearances. The Jonas Brothers allow fans to upload videos and upload they do. There are literally hundreds of videos uploaded. Although the Jonas Brothers haven't uploaded a lot of photos, their fans have uploaded tens of thousands of photos. In addition to connecting with other fans through videos, photos, and the open Wall, the Jonas Brothers keep their Events tab updated with all their concerts and various public appearances.

The Jonas Brothers were among the first to integrate UStream, a live streaming service, and the Facebook Live Chat box into something they called JonasLIVE (see Figure 10.12). Although the Jonas Brothers could have conducted this on their website and still integrated the Facebook Live Chat box, similar to what CNN and the NBA did, the Jonas Brothers chose to hold it on Facebook. In fact, there is even a tab on their page dedicated solely to the JonasLIVE experience.

Figure 10.12   Event Page for a live Jonas Brothers webcast via Facebook and UStream.

In June 2009, the Jonas Brothers held their webcast with the UStream and Facebook Live Chat integration. To help spread the message, a "Share" button was directly below the UStream window encouraging fans to invite their friends. The Jonas Brothers also had a calendar application that you could install on your profile that would keep you and your friends updated on everything Jonas Brothers related.

This was an excellent example of one way that musicians can turn to social media tools to connect directly with their fans. Especially for groups such as the Jonas Brothers, a network such as Facebook serves as the perfect platform to invest time in connecting on.

Gavin Newsom

As of this writing Gavin Newsom is currently the mayor of San Francisco. Mayor Newsom is currently running for governor of California. To help gain support for his campaign, Gavin has turned to Facebook as a main pillar of his outreach. As of September 2009, Gavin has more than 57,000 supporters on his Facebook Page (http://www.facebook.com/gavinnewsom), as shown in Figure 10.13.

Gavin has chosen to integrate a few creative sections into his Page. Gavin has an Add a Supporter widget that adds a widget to your Facebook profile showing your support for Newsom. There is also a link to donate right below the Supporter widget. If you want to donate money to the campaign, it routes to a third-party website that accepts money on behalf of the campaign. But Gavin isn't using the Page only to help spread his campaign message.

Gavin and his team are active on his Page posting to the Wall multiple times per day. These Wall posts consist of everything from summaries of campaign visits to questions asked of the community to promoting sites that they enjoy.

The Newsom team also does well at using the FBML code to create new, custom sections to their Page. Using this coding language, the Newsom team created a

Figure 10.13   Gavin Newsom's Facebook Page. Gavin is currently mayor of San Francisco and also a gubernatorial candidate for California.

"Donate" tab where you can donate directly on the page. They also created a Join tab where you can enter a few pieces of basic information and become a supporter of the campaign. What is interesting on this tab is that they ask you to suggest the Page to friends by linking to it allowing you to easily recommend the Page. Another creative use of Facebook by the team was creating Facebook Captains (see Figure 10.14):

> "Become a Facebook Captain. You'll be the first to know about our Facebook actions and we'll ask for your help on Facebook organizing and fundraising drives and posting campaign updates. It's a great way to help the campaign grow!"

As you can see from that statement alone, Gavin Newsom and his team strongly believe in using Facebook to leverage support for the campaign.

Figure 10.14   FB Captain tab on Gavin Newsom's Facebook Page encouraging supporters to become a Facebook Captain for the campaign.

Besides the custom tabs that the campaign created, they also use the standard tabs quite well. They keep the Events tab constantly updated with all Gavin's appearances and campaign events. A good amount of photos have been uploaded by the campaign team and a couple hundred have been uploaded by supporters.

One section that really sticks out is the "Notes" section. Usually you can blow right by this section if you subscribe to the blog of that particular brand, product, celebrity, or person. It is common practice to have your blog pulled in automatically and posted as a note that then posts to your Wall. It is actually a standard feature with Facebook that it allows you to do without installing any additional applications. But the Gavin campaign has chosen not to use the Notes feature in only this way. Although it does appear that the Gavin campaign pulls in some blog posts from the campaign website (http://www.gavinnewsom.com), it is not the sole source of content in the Notes section. It appears as though original content, not posted elsewhere or pulled in via RSS, is posted in the Notes section.

It will continue to be interesting to see how Gavin Newsom utilizes Facebook as it comes closer to election day and also how he'll continue to leverage Facebook if he does become governor of California.

Vin Diesel

Vin Diesel is an international movie star most well known for the blockbuster movies *The Fast and the Furious*, *Fast & Furious*, and *XXX*. All three movies did very well with a cross section of society. So, it isn't much surprise to see that Vin Diesel is active on Facebook with more than 7.7 million fans as of March 2010.

The reason why Vin was chosen as one of the "Best in Class" is not because the Page is that innovative compared to many of the other Pages that are featured in this book or can be found easily on Facebook. The primary reason why Vin Diesel was chosen is because of how active he is in simply being human. Vin uses the basic features of the platform such as the Photos, Videos, Discussions, and the Wall to communicate directly with his fans and provide them with a behind-the-scenes glimpse of his life (see Figure 10.15).

Vin actively posts approximately once per day or every couple days on his Wall. Vin has uploaded a bunch of photos that are behind-the-scenes shots of Vin filming various movies, at various events, and just hanging out. Vin has also uploaded several videos in which he answers commonly asked questions from fans and talks about his travels or anything else on his mind. Vin also keeps his Events tab updated with all of his appearances such as interviews, public appearances, movies hitting theaters, and more.

What is so different about this Page from many of the others is that it is actually Vin Diesel. It would be easy for Vin to have an assistant manage his presence on

Figure 10.15   Vin Diesel's Facebook Page.

Facebook but instead he does it himself. By doing this he connects directly with his fans. It allows fans to connect with Vin when, if not for Facebook or other social networks, fans would probably never have the opportunity to connect with their favorite celebrity. Granted, Vin is only a single person, so he doesn't have the ability to answer every question or comment that is sent to him. But, just being consistently active, he shows his fans that he really does care about connecting with them.

The Ellen DeGeneres Show

The *Ellen DeGeneres Show* is a daily television talk show that airs to millions of people. Ellen has developed a strong fan base through her show because she appeals to a lot of people and has a diverse listing of guests on the show. It is no surprise that her Facebook Page, as of March 2010, has more than 1.7 million fans.

Although the *Ellen* staff isn't active on its Wall like some of our other "Best in Class" pages, they are very active in keeping the Page updated with new content (see Figure 10.16).

Figure 10.16   The *Ellen DeGeneres Show*'s Facebook Page.

One of the first things you notice when landing on the Page is contest widgets on the home page that constantly change and always have some type of sweepstakes or giveaway that fans can participate in. For those people who are interested in being on the show, the *Ellen* team has created a "Be on Ellen" tab that lists the subjects of upcoming shows (see Figure 10.17). When you click any of the titles, it brings you to a vibrant landing page on the *Ellen DeGeneres Show* website that provides you with a description and has a short form for you to fill out. Just in case you land on that page without coming from the Facebook Page, each landing page actively promotes the show's presence on both Twitter and Facebook.

Figure 10.17 The Be on Ellen tab on the *Ellen DeGeneres Show* Facebook Page allows people to view the subjects of upcoming shows and click through if interested in applying to be on the show.

The *Ellen* team has also created an EllenTV tab that is an extension of the shows blog on its website (see Figure 10.18). The EllenTV tab is perfectly designed to match the look and feel of the show's website. What is really cool is that every blog post has the standard Facebook Share button that allows you to post it directly to your profile, and thus into your stream, or send the post to someone (or a group of people) using Facebook mail. In case you are wondering, this is an active blog with multiple daily posts. Some days there are 5–10 posts providing everything from behind-the-scenes videos to sweepstakes information to show information.

In addition to all this content being shared on the Facebook Page, you can also find a handful of videos from the show and tons of photos that have been uploaded. The *Ellen* team creates a new photo album every month titled "What You Missed in [Month][Year]" with behind-the-scene, funny, or interesting photos from the filming of the show.

The *Ellen* show also has an active Discussion area in which fans regularly talk with one another, offer advice, ask questions, and keep a vibrant community going.

Figure 10.18   The EllenTV tab on the *Ellen DeGeneres Show* Facebook Page is designed to replicate the look and feel of the show's website. Each blog post allows you to share the post with your Facebook community thus extending the reach.

Mashable

Mashable is a popular social media blog that was founded by Pete Cashmore. As of this writing, Mashable is ranked, according to Technorati, as the #3 blog in the entire world. The only blogs that rank higher are the Huffington Post and TechCrunch. One of the reasons why Mashable ranks so high is because it has so many dedicated readers and fans. Besides the blog, Mashable regularly throws parties all over the country and holds a significant presence at a lot of the major social media and technology conferences.

Because Mashable positions itself as "The Social Media Guide," it would come as no surprise that it would have a Facebook Page. As of this writing its Page has more than 140,000 fans.

Mashable uses its Facebook Page (see Figure 10.19) primarily as an outpost for its blog posts. But, because Mashable covers the entire social media space, its posts hit on a variety of topics depending on what's making news on a daily basis. Because Mashable has a deep bench of writers, there are, according to Google Reader, an average of 149 posts per week. What's interesting is that Mashable doesn't use the Notes function but instead posts each new post as an individual update to its Wall. This is beneficial because by doing this it can pull in one of the pictures from its posts or from around its website that Facebook picks up on. This helps to allow readers to quickly scan their Page and stop on posts that might be interesting to them based on the picture, question, title, or conversation taking place.

Besides using its Facebook Page as a way to extend the reach of its blog posts, Mashable provides a lot of information on its Info tab such as the different ways to contact them based on your needs. Mashable also pulls in its Flickr feed and has several videos posted to Facebook. Separate from the Flickr feed, Mashable also

Figure 10.19 Mashable's Facebook Page.

uploads photos directly to Facebook that allows users to easily share these photos, tag themselves or friends, and interact directly with the Mashable team.

The other feature that Mashable uses a lot more than most of the other "Best in Class" Pages is the Events tab, as shown in Figure 10.20. Due to how many events Mashable sponsors, throws, or has a presence at, the Events tab is important for keeping up to date on where its team will be. It also allows for its Facebook fans to note whether they'll attend and help Mashable to spread announcements about its events. This turns into a great networking tool because fans of Mashable can find each other, especially if they live in the same area or attended a recent Mashable event together. This helps to further develop not only just Mashable's community, but the general social media community.

Figure 10.20 Events Page for Mashable showcasing the many events that Mashable organizes and sponsors across the United States.

Similar to how Gavin Newsom encourages you to share the Page with your friends to encourage more supporters, Mashable has a great landing page that encourages you to become a fan. It asks you to first become a fan and then head over to the Mashable Wall so that you can begin interacting with them and other Mashable fans. Because of its following and the relevancy of its topics to its community, there is a lot of interaction on Mashable's Wall. Fans regularly leave comments and "like" posts.

Lessons Learned from the "Best in Class"

Now, your first reaction is probably that everyone that made the "Best in Class" is either a celebrity, politician, or well-known brand. As with their other web presences, you'd expect these groups of people or companies to have well-designed and managed portals. You might not see what you can take away from these various Pages. You are probably wondering why "normal" people and brands weren't profiled.

The major takeaway that you should consider is that all the tools that these celebrities and brands used are all available to you. Many of them are built-in in the Facebook platform. Features such as FBML do require a basic coding skill set, but it's not something that is so far out of your reach to make it impossible. This is what is different with how these people and companies use Facebook versus their many other web presences. Many of us couldn't afford to or don't have enough content to have the scale of website that people such as President Obama, VW, or Gary Vaynerchuk (with his Wine Library site) does. It would either be too costly to build or we simply don't need that many features on our websites. Many websites contain static information that rarely changes. However, Facebook is different because it is constantly evolving. Facebook is real time. The basic features built into the platform allow all of us to integrate various forms of communications tools to reach out and build communities. It is exactly what all those who were featured as among the "Best in Class" have done in various ways. Some have to have teams manage their content for them such as President Obama whereas others get into the trenches themselves and stay directly connected such as Vin Diesel and Gary Vaynerchuk.

The main point here is that all of them use the same tools that all of us can use. They're not receiving special access to features that aren't available to everyone else. The only difference is that their growth rates are much different than the majority of Facebook Pages. Don't get caught up in the numbers, though. Although impressive, they represent only a small portion of their overall fan bases. Also, the size of the number isn't what matters. What matters is having the number of right followers or fans for your brand. Therefore, you should analyze these Pages to see how you can improve your presence or the presence of your brand or your clients' brands. Take segments of what you like from each of these, and other, Pages to create a dynamic presence on Facebook. To help you get started with this analysis, here are five takeaways for you:

1. **Use all available features.** Facebook provides a number of tools that help you to build a solid 360-degree view of yourself or your brand. Use them to their fullest. Upload photos, videos, and events. Interact on the Wall. Share links. Get in there and be part of the conversations taking place.

2. **Try extending your Page with FBML.** As FBML becomes increasingly more popular, we're going to continue to see Pages using the code to make their pages even more unique. Try learning FBML or find a friend or co-worker who might have some coding knowledge. By altering your Page just a little bit away from the standard, you can create a unique experience from the multitude of other Pages that many of us visit on a regular basis.

3. **Promote your page.** Include your Page in your email signature, in your email marketing, on your other social media presences, on your marketing creatives such as brochures, and at any other place appropriate. Come up with creative ways to expose your presence. Gavin Newsom does this perfectly by asking people to suggest his Page to their friends. You can do that too, very easily in fact.

4. **Interact.** If people are taking the time out of their schedules to stop by your Page and leave a comment or upload a picture, you can take the time to comment back. Chris Brogan and Julien Smith spend a ton of time interacting with their fans on their Trust Agents Page. They keep the community active by seeding questions to generate thought and keep the Page top-of-mind with their community. They encourage their community to interact with one another, and they respond to as many questions as they can. This level of interaction is one of the reasons why *Trust Agents* was on the *New York Times* Bestseller list after only two days of being officially released.

5. **Be helpful.** As you build your community, provide members with a variety of types of content and interact often with them; you'll want to be as helpful as possible to them. Being repeatedly helpful to your community can keep members back often. Don't always just promote your stuff; promote others. Share interesting links that are pertinent to your community. Subscribe to some of your fans' blogs, and occasionally promote their relevant posts to the community. Not only will those fans be appreciative, but they'll also be more likely to help promote your Page because it is useful to them.

By combining these tips with your own takeaways, you can start to develop a solid presence strategy for your Page so that you can help to grow it to be as successful as those featured here.

Lastly, there are hundreds of great Pages that aren't mentioned here. If you come across other great Pages that you think we could all learn from, please stop by our community on Facebook and share it. As this book reaches bookshelves, there stands to be tons of new Pages that take these concepts and blow them out of the water. Let us know about them!

11

Shaking the Crystal Ball: What's Next for Facebook

What's next for Facebook drives much speculation across the blogosphere and social media landscapes. At times, there can be so much buzz that it drives mainstream media attention as well. Facebook is held under a microscope that the community uses to analyze its every move. When new team members, especially at the project lead level or higher, joins or leaves Facebook, their previous experience is critiqued and analyzed as to what that might mean for the future of Facebook. Speculation stretches the spectrum starting at the basics of what new features the development team may, or should, be working on to when it will go public. Beyond speculation as soon as a new update is released, a team member conducts an interview, or an announcement is made, it spreads through the blogosphere like wildfire. If it's a new feature implementation, almost immediately you'll find a dozen plus Facebook Pages pop up crying foul on the new features.

This level of scrutiny is expected as Facebook grows at a blistering pace adding hundreds of thousands of new users every day. Facebook is one of the largest websites in the world, and with that comes a life under a high-powered microscope. Also, as social media, as an industry, continues to mature, the entire industry, as a whole, is held under a microscope. Every little move from a social network, large or small, causes a ripple effect of conversations, blog posts, media stories, cheers, and jeers. Rather quickly the community calms down, acclimates to the new feature set, and waits for the next story to drop. With Facebook being the largest social network, it is no surprise that it comes under the most scrutiny.

Besides the scrutiny it comes under by the community, you, as a marketer, should immediately start exploring all new features when they're released to discover how they may be helpful to your activity on Facebook. Of course, not every feature will be useful to you from a marketing perspective. But all new features should be carefully analyzed to see how they may be leveraged to improve your ability to develop, connect, and engage with your community.

In this book, I have laid out a detailed overview of Facebook along with actionable information that can be used personally, professionally, and within your company. By the time you read this book, I would expect several of the features to have changed. That's what makes this chapter the most fun. In the closing pages of this book, I want to try shaking the crystal ball to predict what's next for Facebook.

It is a question that's asked often and one that I want to address. Just as some of the features throughout this book will have changed by the time you read this chapter, I expect that some of these questions will have also been answered. As I was writing this book, one of my predictions for this chapter was going to be that Facebook should acquire FriendFeed. In 2009, Facebook announced the purchase of FriendFeed for approximately $47.5 million. Alas, it is almost impossible to keep up with this speeding bullet that we call a social network. Several times I have revisited the entire manuscript of this book to update stats, features, or other changes made to the network.

Going Public

A recurring question as Facebook continues to grow is whether it will go public. Well, on the surface, all things point to the fact that at some point in the near future Facebook will either go public or be purchased. I tend to think that Facebook will lean toward going public instead of being purchased. First, it is a powerful and large enough company so only a few companies out there could afford to purchase it. Second, there are no reasons for Facebook to want to sell. It's growing at a fast rate on its own, has no problems raising money, and is in the position in which it can actually make purchases of other companies instead of the other way around.

Facebook has already gone through several rounds of funding, with its latest round in May 2009 when it raised a Series D round totaling $200 million from Digital Sky Technologies. All together, Facebook has raised $716 million in five years. It purchased FriendFeed in August 2009 for $47.5 million and Parakey in July 2007. In February 2009, Facebook invested a seed round of $350,000 in LuckyCal, a service that predicts where you're going to be, based on multiple sources of information, and finds useful and entertaining things for you to do while you're there. It's not as if Facebook is only raising funds and making investments and purchases. According to the *Wall Street Journal*, Facebook is expected to bring in revenues of approximately $710 million during 2010.[1]

As if funding, investment, and purchasing information isn't enough, in April 2009 when then-Chief Financial Officer Gideon Yu left Facebook, it started a new search for an executive with "public company experience" at the top of its list of requirements. In June 2009, Facebook announced that David Ebersman would take the helm as the third CFO in three years at Facebook. Previous to Facebook, Ebersman served as CFO at Genetech, a biotech giant, for the four years leading up to its $46.8 billion dollar sale to Roche Holding, according to a *BusinessWeek* article.

Facebook may still be a few years away from an IPO, but all signs point toward going public in the near future. When Facebook does IPO, it is possible, depending on the market conditions at the time, that we could see its stock price rival that of the near untouchable Google.

How does this affect you as a marketer? Well, as someone who just finished reading a couple hundred pages about how you should jump into Facebook with both feet and start allocating your precious time to the social network, any corporate movements—especially moving toward acquisition or IPO—should be of interest to you. Additionally, as Facebook grows larger, either through organic growth, acquisition, or an IPO, potentially tens of millions more people will join the social network. Many of them may be your future or current customers.

Acquisitions

Now that Facebook has acquired FriendFeed, what is the next company that Facebook will purchase? Over the next several months, it will be interesting to see how Facebook fully integrates FriendFeed, its users, and its data into the network. Prior to the acquisition, Facebook had begun to replicate many of the features that had become popular on FriendFeed, such as the live feed, commenting, and likes. So,

---

[1] http://online.wsj.com/article/SB10001424052748704146904574579543239159268.html

it would appear that the foundation has already been set; however, many integration decisions still need to be made before we'll see FriendFeed fully folded into Facebook.

The rumors of Facebook or Google buying Twitter are endless. The rumor seems to pop up once every few weeks and ricochets around the blogosphere for a few days until Biz Stone or Evan Williams, the cofounders of Twitter, do an interview where they state Twitter is not for sale.

It would be a logical next purchase for Facebook but not one that would come easy. With Twitter recently raising another round of funding and reaching a valuation of $1 billion, it wouldn't come cheap. Also, the communities and the way in which these communities communicate on the two networks are very different. There would also certainly be a revolt from the communities.

Another possibility for Facebook would be the acquisition of LinkedIn (see Figure 11.1). Although this isn't a possibility you hear around the industry, it would meet recommendations throughout this book of integrating more features for professionals. An acquisition of LinkedIn would provide Facebook with access to data that it currently doesn't have. It also seems as though the integration of the LinkedIn features wouldn't be too hard because Facebook already captures some of the basics of the information you provide to LinkedIn, such as your work and school history.

Figure 11.1   LinkedIn is a professional social network with approximately 50 million registered users.

Besides the possibility of large acquisitions, Facebook may decide to begin acquiring smaller companies that provide niche feature sets that the network wants to integrate. This is similar to the strategy we have seen from Google over the years. Google has been known for starting to build a new feature and then seeking out a company that it can acquire that does it better. Google then focuses on integrating those features. Using this strategy, Google has made dozens of investments and even more acquisitions. Although Facebook has acquired only two companies and invested in one, it doesn't mean that Facebook may not turn to a similar strategy in the future.

Integrating More Professionalism

One of the fastest growing demographics within Facebook is the 35 to 55+ age group. When Facebook first opened its doors, the features were built around appealing to students. Features such as photo sharing, video sharing, status updates, commenting, and email have become the foundation of Facebook. But as the network continues to grow, it is attracting more adults who want more professional tools and features integrated and more control over how and to whom they share (see Figure 11.2).

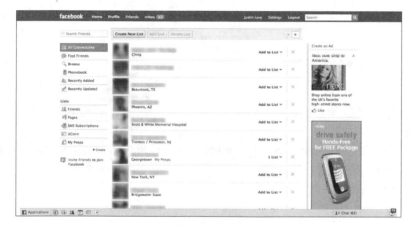

Figure 11.2   Increased control could come through the assignment of sharing controls to Friend Lists.

A complaint that I hear often from professionals is that they need more control over pictures, videos, and other features. They want to limit photos and videos to specific lists. For example, they may not want to show their employees' and colleagues' photos of a family gathering, but they still want to upload these photos to Facebook because they want to share them with their personal network of friends and family. Currently, Facebook doesn't offer this level of control. Users have the ability to control status updates broken into lists, but that's it. The ability to totally control sharing based on lists would be one of those updates that I predict would receive rave reviews from the business community. It would also trigger that community to share more information with Facebook.

Additionally, Facebook should integrate more professional options such as those offered in LinkedIn. LinkedIn continues to be the most popular professional social network with more than 60 million users and growing. LinkedIn enables users to provide recommendations, build an exportable resume, download Vcards, post job announcements and offers several other features that appeal solely to the professional (see Figure 11.3). Although Facebook would continue to grow without integrating similar features, it would reach deeper into its user base if it did. It would keep Facebook users on the network for longer and, in turn, users would share more data with Facebook. Furthermore, it would allow Facebook to continue separating itself from the rest of the pack of other social networks.

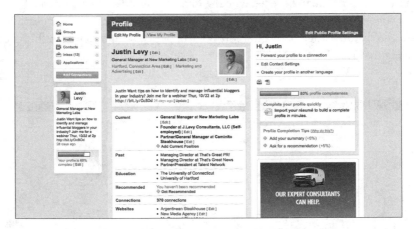

Figure 11.3 A typical LinkedIn profile showing the ability to print your resume and download a Vcard plus other professional features currently missing from Facebook.

Dashboard Customization

Facebook currently allows for minor widget customization on the Profile page. You can move around how your tabs display and where some of the sidebar widgets are located. But, besides those few tweaks, there isn't much customization that is actually allowed. I would like to see Facebook begin to allow for more customization of not only the Profile page but also, and more important, to the Home page.

On the Profile page, it would be great if Facebook allowed the user to customize the look and feel more, similar to what is allowed on Pages using the Facebook Marking Language (FBML). One of the differentiators for Facebook over the years, as compared to its original main competition, MySpace, is the simple and controlled environment that it created. It reminds users of the same experience that they have with Google. Google isn't overloaded with features. Google does have other products that you can choose to interact with, but its main online property does one thing and does it really well. In my opinion, that was one of the downfalls of MySpace. When it began allowing users to add in all sorts of crazy plug-ins, sparkling banners, loud icons, and similar applications, it became unusable, especially from a professional standpoint. Facebook still remains clean and easy to navigate and understand. It should never stray from this, but it could allow for some controlled customization within the Profile area besides just the movement of tabs and some widgets on the left sidebar (see Figure 11.4).

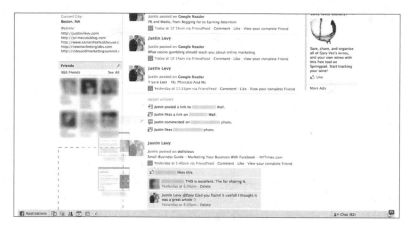

Figure 11.4   The Profile page currently allows for minor customization through the ability to drag and drop.

Facebook has made the Home page your dashboard into engaging and currently has a live feed, a news feed, suggested users, upcoming events, and a few other information sections. However, Facebook doesn't allow you to customize what you see or the location of those widgets on the Home page. I may not want to see a list of suggested users, but I might want to see two different columns of my live feed, similar to the view available in TweetDeck, a popular Twitter desktop client. Alternatively, I may want to see upcoming Events in the top-right corner and outstanding requests and invitations below that.

To allow for this level of dashboard customization, Facebook would need to create widgets that users can choose to integrate. Because it currently doesn't allow for customization of the Home page, users have to deal with whatever Facebook has decided is useful. But, if Facebook allowed for customization, users could choose from a larger selection of options similar to the experience in iGoogle, which has become the main launching pad into the rest of the Internet for millions of users. Google allows you to pull in an endless number of options from RSS feeds, photos, YouTube, news, sports, traffic data, and millions of other possible combinations (see Figure 11.5).

Figure 11.5 iGoogle allows users to fully customize their dashboard with a suite of widgets that allow navigation of Google and the rest of the Internet directly from iGoogle.

Enabling customization would lead to users engaging even more and longer on the network because it would become a source of information for them. Even if the customization weren't as open as iGoogle and allowed the user to choose from only widgets that would provide access from around Facebook, it would still be extremely useful.

The official Facebook iPhone app allows for customized screens and according to some users has become more useful and usable than the web-based version of the network. The iPhone app enables users to add Pages or user profiles to a customized screen to allow for easy access. When you manage or belong to several Pages or Groups, the ability to access these quickly and easily is a huge bonus. The iPhone app doesn't allow for the level of customization that I'm suggesting here, but it is a step in the right direction for Facebook.

It will be interesting to see how future versions of Facebook, along with future mobile versions, will progress to allow for more customization.

Increasing Ways to Connect

Facebook has done an excellent job of extending Facebook into the interwebs with Facebook Connect. Facebook Chat has also become a successful instant messaging service and has been integrated into third-party instant-messaging clients such as Adium, Meebo, and other aggregation services. This enables users to interact with Facebook, even if only through chat, even without being logged into the network. The same affect has happened with Facebook Connect. It has allowed users to use their Facebook profiles to leave comments on blogs, register for access to websites such as the *Washington Post* (see Figure 11.6), and gain access to many other websites. Again, this ensures that you stay closely tied to your Facebook profile as you continue to use it as your main sign-in across the Internet. This is what OpenID has tried to do, but with the popularity and growth of Facebook, it has been a natural extension for the social network.

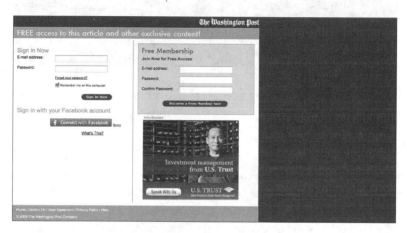

Figure 11.6   The *Washington Post* allows users to connect via Facebook Connect to access most of the newspaper's content.

In the coming months and years, I would like to see more use of these tools across the Internet. As previously suggested, Facebook has the opportunity to distinguish itself as the single login across the interwebs. Along with this, Facebook could provide tools to these websites that could be integrated easily and also have users interacting with the Facebook platform. An example of this would be the Meebo toolbar, shown in Figure 11.7, used on several sites such as Mashable. Besides allowing for drag-and-drop sharing of images and videos, the Meebo toolbar allows users to access their instant-messaging services, including Facebook, directly from the website on which the toolbar is integrated on. Facebook could move forward with something similar but that included tighter integration into Facebook. To do this right though, Facebook would need to provide tools that would be helpful to the website owners and their community. If it were built solely to serve the purpose of Facebook, it wouldn't work as well, more than likely. If it is useful to the website owner, possibly by providing tools that otherwise could be used only by installing multiple plug-ins, Facebook would see a viral effect of the toolbar used.

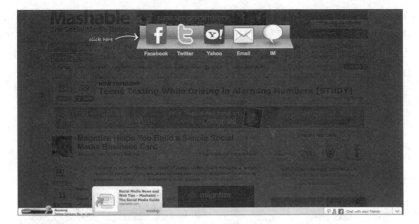

Figure 11.7 The Meebo toolbar featuring chat and drag-and-drop sharing of images, here featured on Mashable.com, a leading social media blog.

Another reasonable addition to the Facebook Chat platform would be the capability for video chat. This has been acknowledged by Facebook as an upcoming feature and may be available as you're reading this. Depending on the feature set included with the video chat, it is possible that Facebook Chat could start to chip away at Skype. Skype has continued to increase in popularity with both individuals and the business community as an instant-messaging service and a cheap way to connect with others via video, also as a substitute for phone service (see Figure 11.8).

Figure 11.8 Skype is a popular instant messaging, video chat, and tool that allows you to make voice calls over the Internet.

Although I don't think becoming a VoIP service is in Facebook's future, one never knows. Facebook does ask you for your contact info and does create a phone book for you from that captured data. Some smartphones and apps have sought to integrate the Facebook contact info into the address book of these devices. However, although this is a possibility for Facebook, it is not one I think they will pursue.

I do believe they will attempt to eat away at Skype and Google Chat with the addition of video chat. With the addition of video chat, Facebook should create a desktop instant-messaging client, though. This is one feature that has fallen down with or decided wasn't needed. Facebook has left it up to aggregator services to provide that service. With a Facebook native application, it could also hook in other aspects of the service allowing the user to interact with it more often, especially if it used Facebook Chat as one of its main instant-messaging services.

An Endless Rainbow of Options

Over the coming months and years, Facebook can and will implement an endless number of features. Some of these will be refreshes of current features whereas many others will be new ways for us to become even more obsessed with the social network. The predictions that I have made are only a few of the many that myself, my colleagues, and our industry discuss on a regular basis. An entire book could be written solely on predictions of what Facebook's next move will be.

Whatever these new features are, I encourage you to review these new features with marketer's eyes. Explore how you can use these features to be more helpful, develop community, and engage your fans, prospects, and customers.

Signing Off

Whether you choose to use Facebook as solely a personal social network to connect with friends and family or you decide to use some of the suggestions throughout this book to help humanize your company and develop, remember that Facebook is just a tool. The real value of Facebook is how you use the various features and build for you and your community.

Facebook is positioned to become the first social network to reach one billion users. With that growth will come more features, more acquisitions, and hopefully, more ways for you and your company to connect with your prospects, customers, colleagues, and fans.

It has been my goal over the course of this book to expose you to the many different ways that Facebook can be used as part of your company's marketing plan. Not all the features or ideas described will be useful for your company. It is my hope though that you have *some* information that will be helpful to you—some information that is actionable and has you eager to finish these last few pages and implement the to-do list you created as you've been reading. The learning doesn't stop here, though.

Let's open this up and have a conversation about everything contained within the book and also all that has changed since the publishing. Please join me over on the community that I created to extend the learning, conversation, and knowledge transfer. Of course, this community is on Facebook and can be found at http://facebook.com/fbmarketing.

I also really want to hear your feedback on the book to help improve future editions and, especially, if the contents of the book has helped you or your company in any way. Feel free to contact me at any time by dropping me a line at justin.levy@gmail.com.

I know that your time is extremely valuable and thank you for spending the time with me that you carved out to read through the book.

Index

Justin R. Levy

#1 BESTSELLER

Facebook

Designing Your Next Marketing Campaign

Marketing

Second Edition

Completely
Revised
and Updated!

 **FREE Online Edition**

Your purchase of **Facebook® Marketing** includes access to a free online edition for 45 days through the Safari Books Online subscription service. Nearly every Que book is available online through Safari Books Online, along with more than 5,000 other technical books and videos from publishers such as Addison-Wesley Professional, Cisco Press, Exam Cram, IBM Press, O'Reilly, Prentice Hall, and Sams.

SAFARI BOOKS ONLINE allows you to search for a specific answer, cut and paste code, download chapters, and stay current with emerging technologies.

Activate your FREE Online Edition at www.informit.com/safarifree

> **STEP 1:** Enter the coupon code: SKPUOXA.

> **STEP 2:** New Safari users, complete the brief registration form. Safari subscribers, just log in.

If you have difficulty registering on Safari or accessing the online edition, please e-mail customer-service@safaribooksonline.com

 Addison Wesley

 Adobe Press

 ALPHA

Cisco Press

 FT Press FINANCIAL TIMES

IBM Press.

 lynda.com

Microsoft Press

 New Riders

O'REILLY

 Peachpit Press

 PRENTICE HALL

 Redbooks

SAMS

 SAS Publishing

 Sun microsystems

 WILEY